Clement Mansfield Ingleby

Occasional Papers on Shakespeare

Being the second Part of Shakespeare the Man and the Book

Clement Mansfield Ingleby

Occasional Papers on Shakespeare
Being the second Part of Shakespeare the Man and the Book

ISBN/EAN: 9783337074593

Printed in Europe, USA, Canada, Australia, Japan

Cover: Foto ©ninafisch / pixelio.de

More available books at **www.hansebooks.com**

OCCASIONAL PAPERS

On Shakespeare:

Being the Second Part of

Shakespeare the Man and the Book.

BY

C. M. INGLEBY, M.A., LL.D., V.P.R.S.L.

LONDON:

Printed by JOSIAH ALLEN, *of Birmingham,*

& Published by TRUEBNER & CO., 57 & 59, *Ludgate Hill.*

1881.

The study of language is passing into a science, but it has no name, other than that given it by Professor Max Müller—'the science of language;' unless we employ that barbarous and vacillating term, Linguistic. For the study of a particular language, without regard to the exact science, we employ the term 'Philology.' The study of the rise and development of the English language is English Philology. It is with a subordinate branch of this that we are now concerned, viz., the phraseology of the Elizabethan or early-modern period, and therein of one of our great formative writers.

A language changes as well from its vitality as from its corruption. The mass of men who employ it, *use* it; *(l'usent)*, *i. e.*, wear it away—corrupt it: [whence then comes its recuperative power? Some would answer, from the influence of exact thinkers and gifted speakers: but the greatest living authority finds that power in spoken dialects, and this view is amply supported by the history of languages over sufficiently long periods. There it is easy to mark the unceasing conflict between Phonetic Decay and Dialectical Regeneration. But during so short a period as the three hundred years covered by modern English, the play of both those factors has been enormously restricted by the influence of literature and education, and there is no doubt that the continuance of this influence will entirely destroy the regenerative power of dialect. The only set-off against decay will then proceed from the best thinkers and speakers, and English will suffer degradation, or else become a purely literary language. Yet during that three hundred years English has undergone, as it is still undergoing,

Contents.

	PAGE
Note	vii
SHAKESPEARE THE BOOK.	
I.—The Tongue of Shakespeare	1
II.—Tests of Authorship	41
III.—Metrical Tests applied to Shakespeare (By F. G. Fleay, M.A.)	50
(Tables on which Mr. Fleay's Essay is founded	99-141)
IV.—The Literary Career of a Shakespeare Forger	142
SHAKESPEARE THE MAN.	
V.—The Elegy on Burbadge	169
VI.—Shakespeare's Play-work	183

Note.

THESE Occasional Papers are intended to complete the series entitled *Shakespeare the Man and the Book.* The entire collection includes such of my smaller writings as I have deemed worthy of preservation. That which here stands first had been deliberately excluded from the first Part; and it owes its appearance here to an after-thought, as having still a purpose to serve by its uncompromising protest against the spirit of emendation, which Mr. Swinburne allows to be one of the three banes of modern criticism.* In order, however, to make it serve a less ephemeral purpose than that for which it was originally written, it was found necessary to make some considerable omissions and insertions, which are here indicated by the stars and the square brackets. The third paper was most generously written for this book to supply the place of my own fragmentary and unsatisfactory notes on Metrical Tests (referred to in Part I, p. 70), of which I have retained the portion constituting the second paper, as a suitable vestibule to Mr. Fleay's edifice. It must not be supposed, however, that I accept all his conclusions, though it is my conviction that whatever of permanent value may be effected in this minor

* *A Study of Shakespeare.* 1880. Page 3.

branch of criticism will be based upon his tables, which for accurate elaboration and sound analysis are greatly in advance of anything that has hitherto been achieved in this direction. I take this opportunity of returning to the learned author of that paper my hearty thanks for his splendid contribution.

As to the rest of the collection, I may say that the fourth paper is as complete a summary of the remarkable facts it deals with as we can ever hope to see; and I can only regret that respect to the living has prevented my dealing here in the same manner, with the more recent and more skilful forgeries which have been a source of corruption alike to the life and the works of Shakespeare during the present century. The fifth paper, though leading up to this subject, barely touches it. It must therefore be regarded as distinct from the contemplated essay.

I had intended this Part to include some further notes on 'Passages Reprieved;' but seeing my way, by extended study and research, to something more important than their reprieve, namely, the definitive settlement of the points that perplex them, I have reserved those notes to form the nucleus of a systematic commentary.

To me the process of investigation, in the pursuit of textual criticism, has no likeness whatever to that haphazard and con jectural chase, which, with a few brilliant exceptions, appears to have satisfied the aspirations of my predecessors. It is not the gallop across country, but the tentative penetration of unfrequented by-ways. The textual critic who discharges his true function is as one who, bearing torch or lantern, attempts to find his way through dark and devious lanes. He seems to himself to be tracing a definite path through the obscurity and to be 'threading dark-eyed night.'* Till this kind of exploration is attempted, and a case of *inert* obstruction is fully established, conjectural emendation is unjustifiable. While the critic is forbidden to force the passage, it is equally out of his commission to turn back until all the resources of discovery are exhausted.

C. M. I.

Valentines, Ilford.
March 25, 1881.

* Even this beautiful image, in *King Lear*, ii. 1, has not escaped without misprint and conjectural alteration.

> *Cornwall.*—You know not why we came to visit you?
> *Regan.*—Thus out of season, threading darke ey'd night.—(Fo. 1623.)

Here the quartos favour us with 'threatening' and Theobald with 'treading;' and that usually sagacious critic remarks, that 'the text as it stands gives too obscure and mean an allusion.' In my opinion it is both clear and dignified, as well as perfectly appropriate.

OCCASIONAL PAPERS

ON

SHAKESPEARE.

I.

THE TONGUE OF SHAKESPEARE.*

WHEN a study is pursued for a livelihood we call it a Profession, and its practice is business. Collateral studies pursued for relaxation, as of the bent bow,—or for amusement, as of inert and easy-going study, we call Dilettantism. There remain yet two worthy ends in the pursuit of knowledge: we may pursue it purely out of love for the subject studied; we then call it Philosophy, Philology, and, pedantically, Philomathy—using the loving prefix *Phil*: or we may exalt into a methodical and exact science, and study it for the discovery of truth; we then call it Logic, Astronomy, Geology, &c.—using the knowing terminals *ic*, *nomy*, and *logy*. This division is of use for marking out the domain of actual science as distinct from those studies which may not lead the student to science.

* From the *Birmingham Gazette* of June 27, July 11 and 25, and August 8, 1867. The principal additions are in square brackets.

great changes. The conflict has been and is between the colloquial and the literary use of the language.] The popular use of words and phrases tends to enfeeble and confound them; to make them less determinate and more general; to make them less discriminate and more vague. By that use words and phrases lose both *intensity* and *precision*. [On the other side of the account is the arbitrary limitation of words to a subordinate part of their meaning, especially of words derived from the learned languages. By that use, too, words and phrases go out of fashion, and ultimately out of use, and others, often less efficient, take their place. We thus acquire, as a set-off against very severe losses, some words of sufficiently clear and precise signification, as well as new idiotisms which in course of time approve themselves to the common sense of the people, and ultimately lose their relations with the personal, the provincial, or the vulgar,

> like the virtues
> Which old wines lose by time.

Meanwhile, as a natural revolt against the laxity of colloquial syntax, the grammatical construction of the literary language becomes more and more amenable to the rules of the pedant. In brief, the language passes into a new phase of its career, and no small impediment is thus placed between its earlier literature and general readers, who employ in their daily life the altered and renovated tongue. For such readers, then, it is almost a necessity that the text of an author belonging to that earlier literature should, to some extent, be confessedly modernized or altered under colour of emendation. In any event it is quite certain that such a text will be modernized in the process of editing—a fact which is perfectly compatible with the duty of printing editions from the ancient texts.]

The Greek language moved by centenarian strides; the Periclean and the Alexandrine epochs, when the language acquired new scope and force, were separated by about a hundred years. Now the English language has moved by bicentenarian strides. Its great epochs are separated by about two hundred years. They are as easily seen as the constellations. They fell in the reign of Edward III, Elizabeth, and George III. Edward III began to reign in 1327, and he reigned fifty years. Around him flourished Wycliffe, Gower, and, greater than all. Chaucer. Elizabeth began to reign in 1558, and she reigned forty-five years. Around her flourished Marlow, Chapman, Shakespeare, Spencer, Sidney, Bacon, and Jonson. George III began to reign in 1760, and he reigned sixty years. Around him flourished Goldsmith, Johnson, Burke, Cowper, Byron, Shelley, Keats, Wordsworth, Coleridge, Southey, Campbell, Scott, &c. Now of all these we have no difficulty in selecting Chaucer, Shakespeare, and Coleridge as those writers who, along with the intercalary Milton and Pope, exercised the greatest influence upon the growth of our mother tongue. Chaucer has been modernized often enough. We have at last become awake to the injustice and danger of this. Bell's edition, Morris's first edition, coming so close on that published by Pickering [and followed of late by Mr. Furnivall's Six-Text Edition], are a pledge that Chaucer shall be righted and henceforth studied in his own language. Some day we shall have Byron, Shelley, Keats, Wordsworth, and Coleridge modernized; but the danger is distant. This danger, which was metaphorically considered in a former chapter, viz., that of an irremediable corruption of Shakespeare, *it stands us now upon* to explain and exemplify. Shakespeare's wrongs are really, though not seemingly, greater than Chaucer's. If a phrase be very ancient and wholly or mainly unintelligible, and a modern phrase be put for it, no one is deceived. In the English New Testament (2 Cor., viii, 1) occurs the phrase, 'We do you to wit of the grace of God.' Wycliffe wrote, 'We maken knowen to you the grace of God,' which, though more ancient by upwards of two centuries than King James's version, is far more intelligible. To forsake the authorized version in this instance, and to write, 'We cause you to understand the grace of God,' is to notify to those who know the older text that we are either retranslating or paraphrasing the passage. But if, instead of this bold modernizing, we were to punctuate the authorized version thus, 'We do you, to wit, of the grace of God;' *to wit* having the sense of namely, or emend it thus, 'We do *preach to* you (to wit) of the grace of God,' without these italics, or brackets, no one but an expert could be sure that this was not the sense, if not the very words, of the old copies. It is this specious, insidious, and stealthy corruption, under the name of 'correction,' that entails the greater mischief; the entire supplantation of the old text is comparatively harmless. Hence it appears the more reasonable course, in the attempt to render Shakespeare intelligible to a later generation, to paraphrase the more difficult passages (marking off the new matter by asterisks), rather than to supersede or alter them under cover of emendation. Recourse, however, is not had to honest and open paraphrase; the gist of the complaint, the essence of the danger, lies in this, that an alloy is secretly interfused with the old text, and an unwary reader is deluded into the notion that he is reading Shakespeare's own words, when he is reading the 'felicitous' substitutes of one who is perhaps contemporary with himself. The surnames of these *cruciatores* or *βασανισταί*, that is to say, *torturers* of Shakespeare, may be very readily determined by the initials C (or K) and B, and by the selection of dissyllables only.* Messrs. Knight, Clark, and Brae have a narrow escape by virtue of the monosyllable: Messrs. *Barron* Field and *Cowden* Clarke, by virtue of the names in Italics not being surnames: Messrs. Halpin and Staunton, by reason of the initial letters. It seems to be on a similar principle that Mr. Ruskin determines who are the greatest painters: the name must not be composite; it must begin with T or V; and the number of vowels or consonants in each must be four; and a man is all the better if he have four of each. The R's seem to have had a very narrow escape. As it is, if they are dissyllabic and the post-initial consonants predominate, they seem to be very nearly of the first class, yet just to miss that distinction: so great is the misfortune of a liquid initial. The G's and H's too look very promising, but the 'sorting demon' does not always work by rule of thumb.

* *Tempora mutantur.* Fresh critics have arisen whose work does not conform to our rule: the worst are not selected, nor are the best eliminated.

The evils of the practice complained of are the more apparent from the frequency with which Shakespeare is quoted. How rarely is he quoted right! In the course of the Waverley novels he must be quoted several hundred times; and yet it is hardly possible to produce a single instance in which the quotation is correct, and generally the errors must have been those of the edition with which Scott was familiar. We need not go to an extreme case—such as Hanmer or Warburton*—to account for the phenomenon. The fact is that very few editions of that day are even tolerable representatives of the old text. The chance is not small that in quoting from one of them you will be quoting Rowe or Theobald. Some years ago a volume was published, called *New Exegesis of Shakspere*, and it was sent to the writer for reviewing. On looking it through (for it was utterly unreadable), the reviewer was struck by the fact that a number of the Shakespeare passages, quoted as illustrations of the author's hypothesis, were not *verbatim* from Shakespeare; and he was to the last unable to discover what edition had been used for that purpose. Even Todd's Johnson gives the passages 'Most *busiless* when I do it,' as an authority for that monstrous compound, and 'doth all the noble substance often *dout*' as an authority for *dout*: and many a writer has gone into ecstacies over Falstaff's 'babbled o' green fields,' without suspecting that he was paying a compliment to 'piddling Tibbald.' †

* Yet how infinitely more sagacious and sensible was the bishop: with all his faults, and they were many and great, he was a conjectural critic of the first class, scarcely inferior to Theobald.

† See De Quincey's *Works* (Black's edition), vol. xiii, p. 119, note.

Even while this article is in hand [*i. e.*, 1867], a new instance presents itself, which is altogether in point. In the May number of the *Cornhill Magazine*, in an article on poetic composition, is an alleged quotation from *Measure for Measure*, iii, 1, which is in these words:

Ay, but to die, and go we know not where;
To lie in cold obstruction, and to rot;
This sensible warm motion to become
A kneaded clod; and the delighted spirit
To bathe in fiery floods, or to reside
In thrilling *regions* of thick ribbed ice;
To be imprison'd in the viewless winds,
And blown with restless violence round about
The pendent world; or to be worse than worst
Of those, that lawless and incertain *thoughts*
Imagine howling! —— 'Tis too horrible!
The weariest and most loathed worldly life,
That age, ache, penury, and imprisonment
Can lay on nature, is a paradise
To what we fear of death.

Not to insist on minor changes, here are two which wholly mar the sense and the construction. Shakespeare doubtless wrote (as the first folio gives) *region* and *thought*. 'Region' is usually altered to 'regions,' because 'winds' is plural, and because the editors have not the faintest notion of the meaning of 'region' in this passage. It is used in the abstract sense (and is therefore almost necessarily singular), and means *stricture* or *confinement*, as that of flies in amber. 'Thought' is usually altered to 'thoughts,' because the editors take it to be the substantive governing 'imagine,' whereas 'thought' is used in the abstract sense, and is governed by that verb, whose nominative is the relative 'that' = who. It may be safely assumed that the sense of this passage, like that of so many others in this author, was shrouded *in tenebris, quæ vix illis lethalibus sunt mitiores*, till the advent of Mr. Hugh Carleton's exposition, which appeared in *The Englishman's Magazine* for November, 1865. Difficult as it is, this speech is incomparably easier than some that occur in the other Tragedies. It would, however, be hard to select a play that better exemplifies the difficulty of our author's diction than *Cymbeline*.* This, it is submitted, is a crucial play, which may well serve as a test of editorial capacity. If an editor fail here, he is certainly no trustworthy editor of the other plays; if he succeed, it is impossible to conceive any mere linguistic difficulty in Shakespeare that would put him to shame. Neither *All's Well that Ends Well* with its multitude of misprints, nor *Timon of Athens* with its legion of corruptions and its complication of double authorship, nor yet *Antony and Cleopatra* with its damaged text and its difficulties of grammatical construction, would serve so well to try and display the varied accomplishments of a really good editor as *Cymbeline*. To bottom some of its speeches is fully as hard as to master an Æschylean Chorus.† Take the following: Belarius, addressing his adopted sons, says:

* In certain technical respects, however, *King Lear* offers a better test of editorial fitness than even *Cymbeline*.

† This was, and is, my deliberate opinion, strengthened only by increased study. It is amusing to compare it with that of the *Times* reviewer of the Cambridge Shakespeare (Sept. 29, 1863), who asserts, without so much as an *opinor*, 'There never was an author who less required note or comment than Shakespeare.' Assuredly, if he be first modernized and improved; but that was not what this writer meant.

Now for our mountain sport, up to yond hill;
Your legs are young: I'll tread these flats. Consider
When you above perceive me like a crow,
That it is Place which lessens and sets off:
And you may then revolve what tales I've told you
Of Courts, of Princes, of the tricks in war.
This service is not service so being done,
But being so allowed. To apprehend thus
Draws us a profit from all things we see:
And often to our comfort shall be found
The sharded beetle in a safer hold
Than is the full wing'd eagle. Oh! this life
Is nobler than attending for a check,
Richer than doing nothing for a badge,*
Prouder than rustling in unpaid for silk.
Such gain the cap of him that makes him fine,
Yet keeps his book uncross'd: no life to ours.

* The folio has 'babe.' *Badge* is one of those very slight and effective alterations of the text, which deserve the name of emendations. The badge was an ornamental cognisance worn by the clients and hangers-on of a great nobleman or courtier, and was valued as people now value a blue or red ribbon. This felicitous emendation was due to the sagacity of Mr. A. E. Brae. A printer's error, indeed, is often wholly unlike the word for which it does duty; but those are cases which render conjecture, however judicious, ingenious and luminous, wholly futile. It is only the small discrepancies which can be conjecturally set right. In one case a most satisfactory emendation was effected by simply restoring the *virgula* of a damaged letter, in another by erasing the *virgula* of a wrong letter, *e. g.*—'flye slow' for 'slye slow' in *Richard II;* and 'sire' for 'fire' in *Measure for Measure;* and some indisputable readings have been made by discovering that *u* or *n* had been inverted, or by some such slight change. This was the only sort of knowledge Zachary Jackson could bring to the business of emendation; but of itself it is not of great use; and that worthy old printer, when he applied it at all, did so very arbitrarily, and with a 'plentiful lack' of success. Observe that when Shakespeare speaks of the crawling beetle he calls him *sharded, i. e.*, covered by his shards: but when he speaks of the flying-beetle he calls him *shard-borne; i. e.*, supported in air by his out-stretched shards.

Whole scenes of such language were poured out in Shakespeare's little theatres before a mixed audience, whereof it may reasonably be supposed the greater part understood what was said. To modern ears there are parts in such speeches which might almost as well be recited in Greek. True it is, however, that modern hearers may catch a meaning from the words; so may modern eyes, that have never read a word of Latin, catch a meaning from some English-looking words in Virgil:*

his Laodamia
It comes; &c.

but it is at least a precarious case, and the chances are that it is *not* Shakespeare's sense that is caught from the recital. If it be not incredible that to the cultivated minds of such men as Rawlegh, Southampton, Spenser, Bacon (if he ever went to the play), Sidney, and a hundred others, the diction of *Cymbeline* was as familiar as household words, we may well apply to that auditory what Whewell so eloquently said of Newton's synthetic method—*mutatis mutandis*—and say: the figurative language of Shakespeare, so effective in his hands, and so effectually grasped by his contemporaries, is often quaint and obscure to us; 'and we gaze on it with admiring curiosity, as on some gigantic implement of war, which stands idle among the memorials of ancient days, and makes us wonder what manner of men were those who could wield as a weapon what we can hardly lift as a burden.'† The position which it has been our aim to substantiate in these preliminary remarks is, that the difficulties which

* *Æneid*, lib. vi. 447-8.

† *History of the Inductive Sciences*, ii. 128.

meet one at every turn in Shakespeare are for the most part due to the fact that Englishmen have outgrown the language of his day, and no longer 'speak the tongue that Shakespeare spoke.'

Typographical errors there are in the text, gross and numerous enough for the entertainment and satisfaction of the most ingenious, the most 'forgetive,' and the most licentious verbal critic that ever guessed. But it is not these which occasion the educated reader of Shakespeare the perplexity which he cannot but feel in every page of those immortal dramas. The main difficulties he stumbles upon there are, we contend, part and parcel of 'the tongue of Shakespeare;' only to be resolved by a diligent and painstaking study of Elizabethan literature and of the history of our language. But instead of a vigorous effort to resolve them, the easy (let us not call it the royal) road of conjecture is struck into, with the same sort of success as attended the trenchant method of Alexander in dealing with the Gordian implements. Editor, commentator, and student find it more conducive to lazy and luxurious entertainment to play the spider rather than the bee. The difficulties of the text are summarily evaded, and the passages which they infest are rewritten, or at least remodelled or recast. Most modern editions of Shakespeare come under this censure, and, whatever may be the opinion of ordinary readers of the bard, it must be owned that in the matter of editorial unfaithfulness the student of the English language and English literature has a genuine grievance.

Let us take an instance: suppose the student were desirous of ascertaining what use (if any) Shakespeare made of 'it'=

its; or 'sith' and 'sithence' = since; or whether he sanctioned the somewhat rare construction of 'no is,' 'no has,' for the negative interrogative; or the interjectional use of 'that'—how few modern editions will help him! 'It' (genitive) and 'sith' are often banished to the shades; and 'No had!' is superseded by 'Had none!' It is often a matter of some importance to support from one author an induction which has been made from another. But if the only editions to which the student has access do not present the peculiarity in question he is led astray in proportion to his confidence in the edition he consults. One of the best instances is that selected by Mr. G. P. Marsh, in lecture xxvi of his *Student's Manual of the English Language* (Dr. William Smith's edition, p. 416). It is an induction from a large quantity of early literature that *sith* was used, like the French *puisque*, as a conjunction of logical sequence (illation); while *sithence* and *since* were specially reserved, like the French *puis*, to express temporal consequence (succession). Now, does Shakespeare conform to this practice? does he corroborate this induction? Mr. Marsh, at the time of writing this lecture, could not consult any of the old copies; and he was rightly suspicious of modern editions, knowing the prevalence of the practice of modernizing the text. He says, in a note, 'I have not cited Shakespeare as an authority for the distinction in question, because, for want of an entirely satisfactory text, I find it impossible to determine whether he constantly observed it or not. Mrs. Clarke's *Concordance* does not inform us what edition was made the basis of her labours; but as she occasionally cites different texts, I presume all those consulted by her agree in this particular point. The *Concordance* gives sixteen examples of the use of *sith*, in all cases as an illative; but *sithence* occurs in *All's Well that Ends Well*, i, 3. in the same sense, as according to Knight's text, does *since*,' &c. What a shift for a teacher or a student to be put to! He cannot lay his hand on a first folio, or Booth's reprint, or Staunton's lithophotographic reproduction: so he has to speculate on the probability of Mrs. Cowden Clarke having consulted more editions than Knight's and Collier's; and on the probability of Knight's and Collier's preserving the old conjunctions. Such is the wretched result of all this unintelligible and unconscientious editing.*

It is no great compliment to say that the Cambridge edition of Shakespeare is the best we have. Mr. Clark, the Public Orator, is a genial scholar; † and his coadjutor, Mr. Aldis Wright, is a trustworthy collator, and a thoroughly good editor: as witness his admirable edition of Bacon's *Essays*. No wonder, then, that this Cambridge edition has been belauded to the skies. Yet it is very far from being a satisfactory edition. Unhappily, its plan is more defective than its execution. Omissions and mistakes there are, but their proportion is small; it is the

* If the reader wishes to see to what an extent this practice of modernizing old authors has prevailed, let him or her consult No. 19 of Messrs. Edmonston and Douglas' *Odds and Ends*. It is a paper, in the style of Dr. John Brown, called *Bibliomania*. We may learn from this that Jeremy Taylor, Milton, and others have fared as badly as Shakespeare.

† Alas! no longer is: he died at York, Nov. 6, 1878, and was buried on the 13th of the same month at Gainford, a little village just opposite his old house. There is an obituary notice of him in the *Academy* of the 23rd.

method upon which these able and conscientious editors have laboured that has deprived their labours of much of their value. Their adherence to the text of the old copies is sufficiently close to have exasperated the veteran innovator, Alexander Dyce; yet they install in their text some words which, as far as we know, were never used by Shakespeare. They allow a considerable license in the conjectural emendation of their own text; yet they leave in a state of *balanced discrepancy* such words as *lunatics* and *windring*. [Nevertheless, in Sonnet 69, last line, 'The solye is this'—they do not so leave 'solye,' but give *soile*: but evidently 'solye' may have been *solve* or *soyle*.] But the faults of the text are nothing compared with the sins of the margins. Say, critic, student, and general reader, to what end do those foot-notes (groaning with their foul charge of monstrous and devilish perversions of the text, gathered with decent and respectful care from the charnel houses of Chedworth, Beckett, and Jackson, and from the dust-bins of Bailey, Keightley, and Bullock) disaster the fair page, and overwhelm in their rubbish the painstaking and conscientious collations of the old copies? One effect they have, and disastrous it is: they serve to bring into suspicion a legion of passages which learning and common sense never called in question; and, by not so much as a ? or a ! (to say nothing of a parallel passage, or a reference to contemporary literature, save in the notes at the end of each play, and these are both few and brief), do the editors ever come to the rescue of the slandered text. [Moreover, the conjectural critic himself has a grievance, since the mere presentment of a conjecture cannot suggest to the most sagacious student the reasons which have induced its author to make it known; and where a conjecture is a true emendation, it may only invite condemnation if it is encountered, for the first time, apart from that explanation and that course of argument which are the factors of its success. I venture to refer to two of my own conjectures, one of which appears in the foot-notes of the Cambridge edition, and one does not. When Timon cries out,

> Take thou that too, with multiplying bans! (*Timon of Athens* iv, i.)

the participle shewed me that Timon is plucking out his hair or his beard: probably, because preferably, the former. But the proposed stage-direction (which will be found in the Cambridge edition, vol. vii, p. 265) cannot demand acceptance apart from the citation of a similar passage in *King Lear*, iii, 7, where Gloster says

> Naughty lady,
> These hairs, which thou dost ravish from my chin,
> Will quicken and accuse thee:

Again in the *Tempest*, iv, 1, where Ariel tells Prospero,

> At last I left them
> I' the filthy-mantled pool beyond your cell,
> There *dancing* up to the[ir] chins, that the foul lake
> O'erstunk their feet,

the very connexion of 'dancing' with 'feet' convinced me that Shakespeare could not have intended to signalise the 'feet' of the three victims, as being less foul to their sense of smell than the scum of the pond—their feet being buried in its muddy bottom. So I proposed to spell the last word *fat*, meaning fit=fytte=dance. How should a reader know what meaning I attach to it if the editor merely enter among the collations and conjectures, '*feat* Ingleby conj.' But even this poor measure of justice would be denied me; for so far as the word 'feat' is concerned I had, unknowing, been anticipated by Mr. Bulloch;* so that if the conjecture had been made known in time, the Cambridge edition would have had simply '*feat* Bulloch conj.' and I should have been nowhere! Meanwhile Mr. Bulloch, when he made the conjecture, had no more notion of the meaning I attach to 'feat' than I had of his 'project'; for he tells us that by 'feat' he meant nothing more nor less than the 'project' of Stephano and his accomplices. I say nothing here as to which is the preferable meaning.] Utterly condemning, then, the plan of the Cambridge Shakespeare, we will assume that we are asked for our notion of a really satisfactory edition for the use of scholars. The following rules, we reply, are for the most part essential and sufficient for the editor's guidance. Whatever other and more detailed directions he may stand in need of, these, in our opinion, are worthy of adoption.

1. The *old text* (with the exceptions which are the gist of 2 and 3) to be reprinted intact.

2. The *orthography* (save in the case of such words as *mo*, *sith*, *sithence*, *porpentine*, *Ariachne*, *sickle* (shekel), &c., where

* Studies on the Text of Shakespeare, 1878, pp. 23—4. See also the Cambridge Shakespeare, vol. i, p. 60, where we find attributed to Mr. Spedding the emendation *fear* (for 'feet') which we know to have been a hantling of Mr. Staunton's. In the above interpolation the first person was naturally used as more to the purpose of a personal explanation.

the old text indicates a more ancient spelling, or a peculiar form, of the word) to be modernized.

3. The *few really valuable various readings and conjectural emendations* of manifestly corrupt words and phrases to be given in the side-margin of each page, with a brief foot-note in explanation and support of each conjectural reading.

4. A *paraphrase*, in the purest and most graceful English (occasionally with Greek, Latin, French, Italian, or German equivalents, according to the requirements of each case), to be given at the foot of the page, for every really difficult sentence.

5. A *commentary*, strictly confined to the elucidation of difficulties due to such obsolete customs and historical facts as are alluded-to in the text, to form Appendix I.

6. A glossary, with explanations, etymologies, and references to the page and line of the text, to form Appendix II.

7. An *apparatus criticus*, with full bibliographical details, and with the editor's reasons for preferring the quarto or folio text, as the case may be, to form Appendix III.

We may further add that, in our opinion, the work should be paged at top, and the lines of the text should be numbered *uninterruptedly* through each play or poem.

Let us now descend from this dry speculation to the more interesting details of textual criticism; and first, by way of making amends for the foregoing *excursus*, our readers are presented with two personal anecdotes. Many years ago, as a raw but 'painful student' of Shakespeare, we were accustomed to make the Rev. W. Harness's one-volume edition the basis of our studies, partly because it was a school-prize, but principally because the only other edition in the house was a villanous curtalled acting edition. Like all young hands, we were impatient of obscurity, and if a phrase was unintelligible, we hesitated not to doctor it in summary fashion, after the example of the Johnsonian commentators. In this enterprising frame of mind we read *Othello*, where (act i, sc. 2) we stumbled at the following passage:

> That thou hast practised on her with foul charms:
> Abused her delicate youth with drugs or minerals
> That *weaken* motion.

Now we had already inferred that in *Hamlet*, where the Prince tells his mother,

> ——— Sense sure you have,
> Else could you not have motion,

'motion' meant *discourse!* A mistake, of course; 'motion' in this passage of *Hamlet* certainly signifying the queen's wanton impulse. That was a curious conclusion, but it rested on a very respectable basis, viz., a fifteenth century book, in which all sorts of head and mind affections were traced to an obstruction or counteraction of the motion of the animal spirits upwards. From this book it seemed very plain that the old physicians believed mind to be the manifestation of an inward motion of this subtle substance. So we readily concluded that in *Othello* the drugs were supposed to have *weakened* Desdemona's mind and judgment. [But, surely, this interpretation would require us to read, with Pope, *notion* for 'motion.' Cf. *Lear*, i, 4—

Either his *notion weakens*, or his discernings
Are lethargied.]

We accordingly altered 'waken' into *weaken*. Years after we found that *weaken* was the word of the old text, and *waken* an emendation by Sir Thomas Hanmer! Similarly, at a later date, we studied *Henry VIII*, in another edition, strong and stronger in the conviction that most, if not all, of Wolsey's speeches were written by Fletcher. Now in act iii, sc. 2, we read—

My endeavours
Have ever come too short of my desires,
Yet *filled* with my abilities.

Our views at that time on the three senses of the verb *file* were vague enough; but as the substantive *file* (list or order) occurred in *Henry VIII*, we let *filed* stand unaltered, but not unquestioned, for the emendation, *fill'd*, we thought worthy of serious consideration. We subsequently found that *filled* was the reading of the folios, and that *filed* was Hanmer's emendation. These, it must be owned, are instructive facts in the literary life of a student of Shakespeare. Endless indeed would have been our toil if we had not obtained some of the old copies; for we should have spent years of delightful leisure in making emendations, many of which we should have ultimately discovered to be outcasts from the venerable old text!

A fatality seems to have beset some passages which are so plain that nothing but their very plainness could have invested 'all their noble substance of [with] a doubt.' Here is one. At the close of that fine passage which occurs at the opening of Act iii, 2 *Henry IV*, the sleepless King says—

> Then, happy low, lie down;
> Uneasy lies the head that wears a crown.

As if this presented a serious difficulty, George Steevens gives a paraphrase of it: 'You, who are happy in your humble situations, lay down your heads to rest! The head that wears a crown lies too uneasy to expect such a blessing.' [He means, of course, to *enjoy* such a blessing.] It is difficult, indeed, to misunderstand the text; but, as we said before, it is not the difficulty, but the plainness which is the source of the doubt. Besides, it were an error to judge of what are called the 'tags' of speeches by the same rules as we judge of the other passages. It was generally requisite, according to the usage of the Elizabethan drama, that tags should sum up the speech, and be in rhyme. For the sake of the former, a conciseness and a boldness of expression was demanded, which strongly contrasted with the rest of the play, and the selectness of the words was often sacrificed to the jingle. These commentators, however, deemed it incredible that Shakespeare should have expressed himself in that manner: so, to it they go. Warburton proposed to read, 'Then happy lowlie clown!' This conjecture was adopted by Johnson; and years after it had been forgotten a gentleman of the name of Cornish offered it as an original suggestion of his own, in *Notes and Queries*, and was aggrieved by Mr. Collier's note on the passage in his *Notes and Emendations* without that conjecture. Then another critic proposed to read, 'Then happy *the* low lie down;' and another, 'Happy *the* low lie down.' At last came a funnier fellow than all. He called to mind that from the substantive *fellow*

Shakespeare derived and employed the adjective *fellowly*. Why not, he thought, have *pillowly* from *pillow*? Steevens had cited the line from Davenant's *Law Against Lovers*—

How soundly they sleep whose pillows lie low.

Besides, *down* is commonly associated by Shakespeare with sleep, [as in *Cymbeline*, iii, 6—

Weariness
Can snore upon the flint, when restive sloth
Finds the down pillow hard.]

So this facetious gentleman wanted to persuade us that Shakespeare in the passage in question wrote

Hence, pillowlie down!
Uneasy lies the head that wears a crown.

That conjecture is *impayable*, and it is a marvel that Zachary Jackson missed it. It would have made him a happier, if not a wiser, man. [Yet there are others to compare with it: such, for instance, as the old corrector's substitution of a stage question, '*Vaughs*' for 'Yaughan' in *Hamlet*, or Professor Leo's suggestion that 'pajock' in the same play is a misprinted stage-direction, '*hiccups*;' or another we have met with in the 176th Sonnet—

Whose worth's unknown, although his *freight* be taken.

i. e., of the 'wandering bark.']

But that's not all about it. Coleridge, under the influence of an extra dose of opium, had suggested that possibly 'low-lie-down' was a compound substantive, serving to designate those wretches who repose on truckle-beds or shake-downs, or under haystacks. He is spoken-of by Mr. J. S. Mill as 'that great seminal writer.' Anyhow this seed, though thrice deserving to perish on stony ground, struck root downward and bore fruit upward, thanks to the tendance of my fellow-townsman, Mr. Eden Warwick. His *Poets' Pleasaunce* (if we remember rightly) contained two lines from one of W. Browne's *Hundred Sonnets*, viz.:

> The humble violet (that low lie-down)
> Salutes the gay nymphs as they trimly pass.*

Here was a remarkable confirmation of Coleridge's conjecture—

> Confirmed, confirmed! O that is stronger made
> That was before barred up with ribs of iron.

But alas! for the success of emendation, however felicitous, and however felicitously supported; Coleridge's ribs of iron were 'false as stairs of sand,' and the corroboration was a

* The following is the sonnet in which the lines in question occur. It stands 6 in the *Visions* of William Browne, which have been printed (from a MS. in the Lansdowne collection): first by Sir E. Brydges in 1815, and lastly by the Roxburghe Library in 1869.

> Downe in a vallye, by a foresti side,
> Neere where the christall Thames roules on her waves,
> I saw a Mushrome stand in haughty pride,
> As if the Lillye's grew to be his slaves;
> The gentle daisy, with her silver crown,
> Worne in the brest of many a shepheard's lasse;
> The humble violett that lowly downe,
> Salutes the gaye Nimphes as they trimly pass:
> Those, with a many more, me thoughte complaind
> That Nature should those needles things produce,
> Which not alone the Sun from others gain'd,
> But turne it wholy to their proper use:
> I could not chuse but grieve, that Nature made
> Such glorious flowers to live in such a shade.

rope of sand. We all know what is the common meaning of the word *garble*. It once meant simply to sift or select. Mr. Eden Warwick's extract from Browne was a selection. In that sense it was garbled. But it was also garbled in the secondary and vulgar sense: for as the lines stand in *The Poets' Pleasaunce*, and as Mr. Eden Warwick sent them to *Notes and Queries* (2nd S., iii, 43), 'the humble violet' was the nominative governing 'salutes,' and the word 'that' was the *demonstrative* pronoun. But in Browne's sonnet 'the humble violet' is the objective governed by a verb which Mr. Eden Warwick has banished to the shades, and 'that' is the *relative* pronoun. In short, Browne wrote—

> I saw . . . the humble violet, that (*i. e.*, which) lowlie down
> Salutes the gay nymphs as they trimly pass.

But the limping angel of retribution was *après ses guenilles*.* It happened on this wise: he had suggested in *Notes and Queries* the possible relevancy of the word *pataikoi*, meaning a hideous face (we believe); and he cited from Bunsen's *Egypt* (1860, vol. iv, p. 228), this sentence: 'This word *pataikoi* has enjoyed a long life; at the present day at Rome, a coin with a hideous or worn-out impression, is called "un pattacco."' Hence Mr. Eden Warwick derives a ray of light for the elucidation of the queer word *pajocke* or *paiocke* in *Hamlet*:

* This quotation from Béranger's *L'Ange Gardien* seems prophetic of the discovery which not long ago vindicated the genuineness of pajocke = patchocke, *i. e.*, tatterdemalion or ragamuffin: applied by Spenser to the degenerate English in Leinster, and by Hamlet to the 'king of shreds and patches.' In our early dramatic literature an Irishman was usually represented or described as an ill-fed, half-clothed, degenerate squatter.

> For thou dost know, O Damon dear,
> This realm dismantled was
> Of Jove himself; and now reigns here
> A very, very *paiocke*.

What word could he possibly mean to put for *paiocke?* Not *pataikoi* * surely, nor yet *patacco*. Doubtless he thought that there was one root from which the Egyptian *pataikoi*, the Italian *patacco (baiocco)*, and the English (?) were derived. What then was the English cognate? Mr. Eden Warwick would have done wisely had he shrunk from the ludicrousness of such a coinage; but he did not (see *Notes and Queries*, 2nd S., xii, 451): and the Cambridge editors have not shrunk from giving him the full credit of the invention. Among the conjectures which have been garnered in its heavily-freighted foot-note we read '*patokie*. E. Warwick. ap. *N. and Q.*' without a single word of explanation.

In an article of the June number [1867] of *The North British Review* an original emendation of a famous passage in *As You Like It*, ii, 1, is naively commended to our favour. On the authority of the folio 1623 we believe that Shakespeare wrote—

> Sweet are the uses of adversity,
> Which, like the toad, ugly and venomous,
> Wears yet a precious jewel in his head;
> And this our life, exempt from public haunt,
> Finds tongues in trees, books in the running brooks,
> Sermons in stones, and good in everything.

The bard has often been praised for his minute and accurate knowledge of nature, and it was never better exhibited than in

* The misshapen gods of Phœnicia.

this passage, for the toad is one of the handsomest fellows in creation: his expectorations are not venomous at all, and his head contains no jewel. Had the critic said as much, and stopped there, all had been well. But he points out that tongues (cured or other) do not grow either on or in trees; that books are not found in water; and sermons, however heavy, are not found in stones. So he proposes to read:

> Finds *leaves on* trees, *stones* in the running brooks,
> *Sermons* in books, and good in everything!

We shall now request our readers' attention to some of the curiosities of the text itself, apart from the speculations and mistakes of his editors. Where the structure of thought is involved and perplexed, especially where inversions and other indirect expressions are employed in the communication of thought, there is imminent danger of saying the opposite of what is meant. De Morgan found this danger so great, and the unaided powers of the individual mind so unable to cope with the possible cases which it might be called upon to analyse, that he invented a new logical system to supply the want. This he called *The Logic of Relations;* and it must be owned that its publication has done philosophy at least one good service —viz., it has opened up a new lode of logical inquiry, and demonstrated the purely artificial character of that horizon which, from Aristotle to Hamilton, had been held to be the limit of formal thought. By the aid of De Morgan's *Logic of Relations* the feeblest understanding might securely combine the most abstruse relations of persons and things; it would be to the thinker what musical grammar is to the composer, or what algebraic art is to the mathematician.

But occasionally a writer is guilty of the sort of blunder above indicated, in a phrase of the simplest structure; and we are then obliged to credit him with slovenly thought, or want of thought. At the same time, we must not bring such accusations against a writer of established merit, without carefully considering the possibility of our having mistaken him; of our having missed the sense of an archaic word or phrase; or, worse, of our having imputed to him the less probable of two possible senses which the passage in question may bear. For instance, in Ben Jonson's charming lyric, *Drink to me only with thine eyes*, we meet with a phrase of this sort:

> And might I of Jove's nectar sup,
> I would not change for thine.

If this be an ellipsis for,

> I would not change Jove's nectar for thine,

in the sense of substituting the one *for* the other, it says the very opposite of what the poet meant. Clearly enough, he meant to say, that so greatly did he prize the nectar of the lady's lip, that he would rather forego Jove's nectar than lose the lady's. But this very attempt to fix a solecism on the great grammarian of the seventeenth century (whom we cannot but regard as a foreshadowing of another Johnson, of the eighteenth) shows us that it is we that are wrong, and not Ben. He says he would forego Jove's nectar *for* the lady's; that having the lady's, *for* that he would not desire a change. Such, we contend, is the meaning of the line: at the same time we must own that at best there is a little fogginess in the construction, and, like many other time-honoured things, we wish it had been otherwise, holding that such a form would have been 'more honoured in the breach than the observance.' Cf. a similar inversion in *Cymbeline*, iii, 4, which we give later on.

It is interesting to inquire whether Shakespeare was ever guilty of the offence charged on Ben Jonson. Can we find in his plays any instance of this solecism? The first that occurs to us is 'as right as a trivet,' and we only notice it because it occasioned a friend of ours the greatest perplexity. He is by no means *omnibus horis* a fool; and in his more lucid intervals he would not have put this down in the list of passages which express the opposite of what must have been designed by the writer. This is the passage:

> The murkiest den,
> The most opportune place, the strong'st suggestion,
> Our worser genius can, shall never melt
> Mine honour into lust, to take away
> The edge of that day's celebration,
> When I shall think, or Phœbus' steeds are founder'd,
> Or night kept chain'd below.—*Tempest*, iv, 1.

Said our friend, evidently wool-gathering, 'Surely Ferdinand does not mean so poor a compliment to the charming Miranda as to anticipate too protracted an enjoyment. He must have meant to say that his wedding-night would seem "brief as the lightning;" as if Phœbus' steeds had run away with Phäethon, bringing back day before it was due.' He was all the while fancying that Ferdinand is including the night of consummation in the day of celebration, which otherwise would seem as much too long as the former seemed too short.

The beginning of the Duke's speech in *As You Like It* (act ii, scene 1), from which we have already quoted, contains another seeming example of the kind of solecism we are considering.

> Here feel we not the penalty of Adam,
> The seasons' difference, * * *
> * * * these are counsellors
> That feelingly persuade me what I am.

This speech being punctuated so as to connect 'the penalty of Adam' with 'the seasons' difference,' the Duke is made to say that he and his co-mates do not feel the seasons' difference, in the same breath with his admission that he does feel it, and draws a moral from it. [It is almost impossible to doubt that there is something wrong with the old text; and it is rather a relief than a satisfaction to adopt the emendation of Theobald, and read *but* in lieu of 'not' in the first line.]

In the same play, act ii, scene 7, we have a still more striking instance, where Jacques is made to say—

> He that a fool doth very wisely hit,
> Doth very foolishly, although he smart,
> Seem senseless of the bob; if not,
> The wise man's folly is anatomis'd
> Even by the squandering glances of the fool.

The editors have, in our judgment, here 'done very foolishly'—they follow Theobald in reading

> Not to seem senseless of the bob,

a reading which puts the complementary words 'if not' in a difficulty, and disturbs the balance of the antithesis. Moreover, we do not think they have made out a case for verbal emendation. It is surely just because simulation and dissimulation are so inherently foolish that the fool does wisely in his squandering glances or random shots. 'Doth' in both places is the auxiliary.

A still more remarkable instance occurs in *Cymbeline*, act iv, scene 2, Belarius says of Cloten :

> Being scarce made up,
> I mean, to man, he had not apprehension
> Of roaring terrors ; for defect of judgment
> Is oft the cause of fear.

Now this appears to state the very reverse of what must have been meant. If Cloten, from the inexperience of youth, had no apprehension of terror, his defect of judgment was the cause not of fear but of fearlessness. The editors, assuming that there must be a misprint somewhere in the last clause, propose various expedients for getting over the difficulty: some read, *th' effect*, or *the act*, for 'defect'; others, *cure*, *sauce*, or *cease*, for 'cause ;' while others wisely leave the text to shift for itself.*

We have another instance in *Hamlet*, act i, scene 3, where Laertes tells his sister that

> The chariest maid is prodigal enough,
> If she unmask her beauty to the moon.

* For the discussion of the first, and the complete resolution of the second and third of these critical difficulties, we beg to refer our readers to *Shakespeare: the Man and the Book*. Part I. 1877. Pp. 138–140.

Very beautiful, indeed, is that last line; but the penultimate line might almost mean the opposite of what it says, for the very force of Laertes' counsel is that the maiden who is *least chary* of her favours is prodigal of them if she but unmask her beauty in sight of the chaste and cold virgin-queen of night. But, after all, 'the chariest maid' gives excellence sense if we understand (by ellipsis) the words 'such as I wish you to be,' *i. e.*, I wish you to be so ultra-scrupulous that you are prodigal enough of your charms, if you shew them to the moon. So we have not yet found an indubitable case in which Shakespeare has said the opposite of what he must have meant. Let us seek further. In *Julius Cæsar*, iii, 1, after the assassination of Cæsar, Mark Anthony enters and begs his death of Brutus and the rest. To this Brutus replies:

> For your part,
> To you our swords have leaden points, Mark Antony:
> Our arms in strength of malice, and our hearts
> Of brothers' temper, do receive you in
> With all kind love, good thoughts, and reverence.

Now, if their hearts had brothers' temper, their arms certainly had no strength of *malice*. The seeming contradiction has been overcome by assuming a misprint in one part or other of the third line: some conceiving that 'in' is an error for *no;* others that the error lies in both the words 'in strength;' but the more probable hypothesis is Singer's—that 'malice' is a misprint for *amitie:* a conjecture for which very much may be said.

What are we to make of the following, from the play-scene in *Hamlet* (act iii, scene 2), where the Player-Queen says—

Yet, though I distrust,
Discomfort you, my lord, it nothing must:
For women fear too much, even as they love;
And women's fear and love hold quantity,
In neither aught, or in extremity.
Now, what my love is, proof hath made you know;
And as my love is siz'd, my fear is so.

The phrase *to hold quantity* means to have great proportions. It is used by Shakespeare in one other place, viz., *A Midsummer Night's Dream*, i, 1:

Things base and vilde *holding no quantity*,
Love can transform to form and dignity.

The Player-Queen then says, plainly enough, that women are jealous and mistrustful, because their fear and love are always great: and that either is so for one and the same reason—the jealousy of monopoly. To point this, she should have added:

In either [women are] naught, or in extremity.

or

Either is naught or in extremity.

i. e., neck or nothing. But this she is far from saying, and the oversight (if such it be) has been suffered to remain untouched.

At the same time it should be kept in view that the phraseology and prosody of the Interlude are to be judged by a very different standard from that which we usually employ in dramatic criticism. Both in the Interlude and in the speech on 'The rugged Pyrrhus,' if, indeed, these parts of *Hamlet* were from his pen, Shakespeare's object was to place his versification in the strongest possible contrast to the rest of the play, and in doing so to invest those parts with such a quaintness, stiffness, and formality as to give them the appearance of a higher antiquity. In an adequate representation of this singular drama the effect is marvellous. The contrast thus obtained and the unreal and artificial character of the Interlude plays off upon the spectator the unconscious impression that the Danish court is a reality, and that he is witnessing, as in a magic mirror, a transaction of real life.

De Quincey, in his eloquent paper on 'The Greek Tragedy,' has given us an admirable criticism on this subject. If his theory be correct, the Interlude in *Hamlet* serves an opposite end to that obtained by the Greek chorus. The chorus, being in a closer relation to the audience than are the *dramatis personæ*, serves to deepen the effect of the drama, and to throw back its action into a mystic abysm of time; while, on the contrary, the antique Interlude in *Hamlet* serves to invest the main play with all the attributes of contemporary life. Somewhat of the same effect is produced by the ravings of Ophelia and of Lear. When once we discern the truth of those awful and affecting freaks of 'lawless and incertain thought,' and are brought into sympathy with the persons afflicted, there is forced upon us an increased perception of the reality of that *sane* drama, to which they are the dreadful exceptions.

In judging, then, of such a line as

> In neither aught, or in extremity,

we must consider whether the expression which offends us be not an intentional piece of archaic *gaucherie*. Unfortunately, we cannot now settle the question. In relation to the foregoing remarks on the Interlude may be studied with especial profit the longer speech of the Player-King, from which we give the following extract:

> Purpose is but the slave to memory:
> Of violent birth, but poor validity,
> Which now, like fruit unripe, sticks on the tree;
> But fall, unshaken, when they mellow be.
> Most necessary 'tis that we forget
> To pay ourselves what to ourselves is debt;
> What to ourselves in passion we propose,
> The passion ending, doth the purpose lose.
> The violence of either grief or joy
> Their own enactures with themselves destroy:
> Where joy most revels, grief doth most lament;
> Grief joys, joy grieves, on slender accident.
> This world is not for aye; nor 'tis not strange
> That even our loves should with our fortunes change;
> For, 'tis a question left us yet to prove,
> Whether love leads fortune, or else fortune love.
> The great man down, you mark, his favourite flies;
> The poor advanc'd makes friends of enemies.
> And hitherto doth love on fortune tend:
> For who not needs shall never lack a friend;
> And who in want a hollow friend doth try,
> Directly seasons him his enemy.

This long digression, which has little or no bearing upon the plot of the Interlude, must have wearied the treacherous Queen not a little: as we fear it hath wearied our readers. But it is well sometimes to read that passage apart from the play, that we may fully realize the sententious formality which characterizes and differentiates the text of 'a play within a play.'

In these extracts from the Interlude there is hardly an observation which may not serve to manifest the *differentia* of the two styles of composition by Shakespeare in *Hamlet*. Nearly every observation is literally an abridgment, and therefore a compression, rather than an expression, of the poet's thought. For instance, 'The great man down, you mark, his favourite flies,' is a phrase which seizes the *last* fact in the great man's career, and its *immediate* consequences on his favourites; and the two things are connected in an extremely curt and inelegant manner. Down comes he, then off go they, is its substance. But when Shakespeare is writing for the modern drama, how differently does he deal with the inconstancy of favourites. In *Timon of Athens*, scene 1, the *Poet* at once points a moral and paints a picture, when he says—

> When fortune in her shift and change of mood
> Spurns down her late beloved, all his dependents
> Which labour'd after him to the mountain's top
> Even on their knees and hands, let him slip down,
> Not one accompanying his declining foot.

Again, in *Henry VIII* (act iii, scene 2), Buckingham says—

> Yet you that hear me,
> This from a dying man receive as certain:
> Where you are liberal of your loves and counsels,
> Be sure you be not loose; for those you make friends,
> And give your hearts to, when they once perceive
> The least rub in your fortune, fall away
> Like water from ye, never found again
> But where they mean to sink ye.

Here, however, the author almost certainly is Fletcher, not Shakespeare.

[There are many other cases in point, besides the few which I have given, occurring up and down the text of Shakespeare. In *Hamlet*, iii, 1, Rosencranz says that Hamlet was

> Niggard of question, but of our demands
> Most free in his reply.

Now the fact was, as the play obtrusively shows, that the prince was 'most free in his questions,' but to their demands 'niggard of reply.' Of course I do not pretend to reconstruct the lines in a metrical form. Again in *Hamlet*, iv, 7, the King replies—

> —— If it be so, Laertes,
> As how should it be so? How otherwise?

But he should have said

> —— If it be so, Laertes,
> As how should it not be so; how otherwise?

In *Cymbeline*, iii, 4, Pisanio tells Imogen, when she acts the man,

> You must forget to be a woman; *change*
> *Command into obedience: fear and niceness,*
> (The handmaids of all women, or, more truly,
> Woman its pretty self) *into a waggish courage:*

but if she were bid to 'change fear and niceness into a waggish courage,' she must be bid to 'change obedience into command.'*

In *Winter's Tale*, i, 2, we read

> Whereof the execution did cry out
> Against the non-performance.

There 'performance' seems to be meant.]

* For a similar passage, see *ante*, p. 27.

A writer who aims at anything like completeness in an essay would assuredly eschew such a subject as ours. Such an essay would rather be an interminable treatise—a sort of 'story without an end.' We have already considered one peculiarity of the text, viz., that of expressing (in appearance, at least) the reverse of what must have been meant. It is remarkable that many a word has changed its meaning and passed over to one which is the reverse of what it once signified, and some words even retain two opposite meanings at once. To *let* still means to *hinder*, as well as to *permit*. To *check* now means only to *restrain*, but it once meant far more than this, viz., to *direct*. The check-string of a close carriage is simply a string attached to the coachman's arm, by pulling which he is instructed to stop. This is, indeed, a very limited use of a check-string. An eminent London physician had two check-strings to his carriage, whereby he actually guided the driver. A pull at the right string made the driver turn to the right; and *mutatis mutandis*, as to the left string. By pulling both at once he was made to stop. This gives us a notion of the ancient meaning of the verb to *check*. To *prevent* is used in the Book of Common Prayer in the sense of *lead the way*, though at present it has no other meaning than *obstruct*. The adjective *secure* now means *safe*, but it once meant *careless*, and by implication, *unsafe*. Shakespeare uses not only the adjective in that sense, but also the verb *secure* in the sense of *render careless* or *put off guard*. As to the great majority of such words, the cause of the change of meaning is in the root of the word. But it is quite conceivable that mere carelessness and inaccuracy in literary composition, as well as in colloquy, should have conduced to the change in some instances. It has been made a question how the verb *help* ever came to mean *control*. Yet nothing is more certain than that at the present day we use the verb *help* both in the sense of *aid* and in that of *control*. 'Why do you wink your eyes so?' a mother asks of her child. The child naturally replies, 'Because I can't help it, mamma.' Mamma might say, 'My dear, if you did not help it, it would not take place;' and the infant, having no knowledge either of philology or of ganglionic action, would be nonplussed.* Now, *behove* or *behoove* meant exactly the same as *help;* and oddly enough, we find Shakespeare using it in the sense of *restrain*. Of course his editors will not allow this, so they alter it to *behave*, which is a cognate form.

Poets have ever been privileged to generalize on a faculty or sense, and apply it figuratively to any object, animate or inanimate. For instance, Dante, in the *Inferno*, canto v, l. 28, says—

> Io venni in luogo d'ogni luce muto,

i. e., I came into a place, where all light was silent. He has a similar phrase, viz., '*dove 'l sol tace*,' in the same poem, canto i, l. 56. Milton imitates this in *Samson Agonistes*—

> The sun to me is dark,
> And silent as the moon
> When she deserts the night,
> Hid in her vacant interlunar cave.

* Professor De Morgan contended (in the *Athenæum*) that we ought to say, 'I shall not go if I *can't* help it,' not *can* help it. But 'help' there means prevent, because it once meant *cure*, as of an evil act or state.

Which Shelley imitates, in turn, in *Prometheus Unbound*, but giving the moon, more appropriately, the sense of sight rather than of speech—

> and by what secret spell
> The pale moon is transformed, when her broad eye
> Gazes not on the interlunar sea.

We are pretty sure the notion of the silent sun, or silent moon, is classical. In a work called *Scriptores de Re Rustica*, 1543, occurs the phrase *silenti luna* (quoted in Edmondstone and Douglas's *Odds and Ends*, No. 19) and probably something like it will be found in Ovid or Virgil. Sophocles, in his *Œdipus Rex*, l. 381—2, in lines which sputter with t's, predicates blindness of a man's ears!

> ἐπεὶ
> τυφλὸς τά τ' ὦτα, τόν τε νοῦν τά τ' ὄμματ' εἶ.

Odd as this is, Milton comes near it when he predicates blindness and prehensile power of the mouth:

> Blind mouths, that scarce know how to hold
> A sheephook.—*Lycidas*.

There, however, *mouths* is figuratively used for preachers, and *blind* for lewd or dull.

[Wordsworth speaks of a *deaf and silent* eye in his *chef d'œuvre*.

> Thou best philosopher, who yet dost keep
> Thy heritage, thou Eye among the blind,
> That deaf and silent, read'st th' eternal deep, &c.—
> *Ode on the Intimations of Immortality*.

We have *hearing eyes* in Shakespeare's Sonnet 23 (last line)—

> To hear with eyes belongs to love's fine wit,

and the converse, a *seeing ear* in Poe's appreciative and discriminate critique on Tennyson :

> He seems to see with his ear.—
> *Democratic Review*, N. Y., Dec., 1844, p. 580.]

All this is (what used to be called) *propheme* to the statement that Shakespeare makes a sound fragrant, if he does not exactly invest the ear with the sense of smell:

> Oh ! it came o'er my ear like the sweet sound
> That breathes upon a bank of violets,
> Stealing and giving odour !—*Twelfth Night*, i, 1.

Of course Shakespeare cannot be allowed to tell us that one hears the fragrance of a sound ; so the critics come to the rescue. Rowe gives us *wind;* Pope, *south ;* and others, *sou' wind*, *scent*, and *sough ;* not one of which really gets over the difficulty of anything odorous affecting the ear. As to *scent*, that makes matters worse, unless we read

> Oh! it came o'er my *nose* like the sweet *scent*, &c.,

which no one as yet has had the temerity to propose; and *sough* is in the same predicament with *sound.* [One is reminded that in *Twelfth Night*, ii, 3, Sir Toby puns on the epithet 'sweet,' and says, 'To hear by the nose, it is dulcet in contagion.' But it would require the inexhaustible industry in research of Mr. Francis Jacox to complete the tale of such instances.]*

* The rest of the original paper, relating to the subject of verbal jingles, quibbles, and puns (which would seem to justify distinct and systematic treatment), was not thought worth reprinting.

II.

TESTS OF AUTHORSHIP.*

THE fourth chapter of *Shakespeare, the Man and the Book*, will to some extent serve the purpose of shewing the state of the case before the advent of Hertzberg and Fleay, and the application of numerical tests to the text of Shakespeare. It is, indeed, true that the subject of metrical tests had emerged before the date at which that chapter was delivered as an oral address, and had engaged the attention of Bathurst, Spalding, Hickson, and Spedding; but within the compass of such a paper it was obviously impracticable to treat of a new and intricate method of criticism. That chapter, then, may serve and will stand as preparatory to the following brief sketch of quantitative tests of authorship.

What are usually called æsthetic tests are qualitative only, and it is on these that we have been wont to rely. Now it must be understood at the outset that, just as these internal evidences of authorship cannot dispense with the external—that is, with those which connect Shakespeare's works with a historical personage known to us in other relations—so the quantitative tests, however powerful and searching, cannot

* These remarks on tests of authorship are here given as an introduction to the essay on the application of certain of them to the traditional works of Shakespeare, written expressly for this volume by the Rev. F. G. Fleay.

dispense with the qualitative (which appeal to a much higher faculty of judgment), nor yet with the general law of mental development by which we are entitled to look for riper wisdom, fuller knowledge, purer taste, and greater command of language at the later than at the earlier period of the poet's life. The notion that we can treat his works as a mathematical problem, and ignore all other considerations but those which admit of exact numeration, is too absurd to have been ever seriously entertained.*

* THE LATE MR. C. BATHURST'S CLASSIFICATION.

1. External and direct evidence of date. (Higher limit.)

2. Allusion (supposed) to an event the date of which is known. (Lower limit.)

3. Induction from differences of style [and metre]. 'Though the changes of style in different periods of his life must not be assumed, but proved from actual dates, yet when the fact of such change in general is well established, we may infer some few individual dates backwards, from those general rules.' (*Remarks on the Differences in Shakespeare's Versification.* 1857. P. 1—2.)

MR. J. W. HALES' CLASSIFICATION.

1. External evidence (of date).
2. Historical allusions in the plays.
3. Change of metre.
4. Change of language and style.
5. Development of dramatic art as shown in power of characterization.
6. The like as shown in dramatic unity.
7. Knowledge of life.

(*Lecture on Shakespeare: Academy*, January 17, 1874.)

MR. A. W. WARD'S CLASSIFICATION.

A. EXTERNAL TESTS.

(*a*). *Mention* in other works.
(*b*). *Allusion* in other works.
(*c*). Date of first known publication, Stationers' Registers.
(*d*). Mention of plays *as new.*

B. INTERNAL TESTS.

(*a*). Allusions in the plays.
(*b*). Style.
(*c*). Versification;
1. Rhyme (indic. early date).
2. Stopt and unstopt lines.
3. Feminine endings (redundant syll.)
4. Weak endings.

(*d*). Mental tests:
Artist's progress: construction: characterization: taste: human pathos: self-control: moral purpose: power of thought: views of life, death, eternity.

(*History of English Dramatic Literature.* Vol. i, pp. 357—365.)

The internal evidences of authorship, then, are either qualitative or quantitative. The latter are either verbal or metrical. The possibility of testing authorship by the comparative richness of the vocabulary was, I believe, first pointed out by Professor De Morgan, whose communication on the subject to *Notes and Queries* appeared in 1st S., xii, 181. It was taken up by other correspondents whose notes, together with a second by De Morgan, appeared in the same periodical, 1st S., xii, pp. 269, 309, 332, 409, and 410. The proposal of De Morgan was based on 'the law of average:' which he thus enunciates: 'however uncertain the individual cases may severally be, one set of a thousand will generally bear a considerable resemblance to another; still more so one of ten thousand to another set; and so on.' He adds,

> Of all easy tests, perhaps the easiest is the *average number of letters in his word.* There is no doubt that some writers have a natural preference for longer words than others. If the law which has never failed elsewhere should hold true here, we are to expect that if, upon one ten thousand consecutive words taken from each author, Johnson should show, one word with another, a quarter of a letter per word more than Addison, the same result, or one very near it, would occur in another ten thousand taken from each writer. A writing attributed, but falsely, to an author, might possibly be detected by its average word exhibiting such a difference from that of the indubitable writings, as never appears between those undoubted writings themselves.

According to this proposal, though no amount of agreement would prove identity of authorship, a sufficient want of agreement would negative that identity. Mr. R. W. Hackwood, having applied De Morgan's test to eight selected authors, on six thousand words in each (500, 1000, or 2000 being consecutive), obtained the following results.

Name of Author.	Average number of letters in his word.	Name of Author.	Average number of letters in his word.
Scott	4.799	Goldsmith	4.463
Hitchcock	4.773	Addison	4.287
Dickens	4.568	Gough	4.208
Irving	4.502	Halliburton	3.907

Another correspondent (A. F. B. of Diss) instead of counting the number of letters per 500, 1000, or 2000, counted the number of words of 1, 2, 3, etc., up to seventeen letters, respectively, and obtained the following results.

Name of Author.	Average number of letters in his word.	Name of Author.	Average number of letters in his word.
Gibbon	4.875	Milton	4.501
Junius	4.630	Burnet	4.396
Burke	4.626	Butler	4.220
Cowper	4.539	Swift	4.205
Keats	4.515		

These tables, which serve well for examples, cannot be relied upon for critical purposes; but evidently, as De Morgan pointed out, if tables, on a sufficiently large basis, were prepared from the known authentic writings of Francis, Burke, and the other of the forty-five or forty-six candidates for the honour or dishonour of having written *The Letters of Junius*, we should be able, beyond question, to eliminate the ruck, and select the few writers whose claims deserve exact and thorough examination.

It will now be obvious that this kind of test is applicable to the determination of the chronological order of a single writer's works. As he grows in knowledge and experience, he acquires the use of a richer vocabulary of synonyms, and from the judicious employment of classical equivalents may be expected to show a higher number of letters in his average word. I am not aware that this test has ever been applied to Shakespeare, but it is evident to any one acquainted with his works that the average for *Macbeth* or *Troilus and Cressida* would be greatly in excess of that for *A Midsummer Night's Dream* on the one hand, and that for *The Winter's Tale* on the other. To say the least, the application of this test to Shakespeare might be used as a check on the results derived from other tests.

So much for De Morgan's proposed test of 'the average number of letters in an author's word.' Another correspondent of *Notes and Queries*, 'Avon Lea,' proposed a somewhat different test: viz., 'the kind of letter most in request by different authors.' To ascertain this 'the easiest way (he says) would be to have 2600 small cards, apportioning 100 to each letter, on which it should be printed, or written in printing letters. Then a box should be provided, divided into twenty-six portions, one for each letter, and labelled. By this means, when the 100 of letter e were exhausted, the fact could be easily noted down, and so on with the rest.' The same end might be otherwise attained by sorting 'pie' into an empty case. He records the fact that in a 'fount' of type, the number of letters of each sort are as follows:—

e	1200	u	340	q	50
t	900	c	300	j	40
a	850	m	300	x	20
n	800	f	250		
o	800	w	200	fi	50
s	800	y	200	ff	40
i	800	g	170	fl	20
h	640	p	170	ffi	15
r	620	b	160	ffl	10
d	440	v	120	æ	10
l	400	k	80	œ	6

I do not know if this proposal has been applied to any author.

Metrical tests have been variously classified: indeed, the subject is so new that it is not possible at present to give them an objective treatment. The following are the more important of them.

Old Tests	I.	Final extra syllable, or female ending.
	II.	Stopt line.
	III.	Rhyme.
	IV.	Middle cæsura.
	V.	Light or weak ending.
*New Tests	VI.	Alternate line.
	VII.	Doggrel.
	VIII.	Short or broken line speech ending.
	IX.	Alexandrine.
	X.	Middle extra syllable.

* Proposed by Mr. Fleay. See his *Manual*. 1879. Part ii, chap. i.

Besides these many others have been proposed; *e. g.*, the 'tag-rhyme test,' the 'initial trochee test' and the 'middle trochee test,' all proposed by Mr. Fleay; the 'pause test' proposed by Mr. Spedding; the 'more prose test' proposed and subsequently withdrawn by Mr. Fleay. Two tests of another sort, the 'prevalent word test,' and the 'choric reflection test,' were proposed by myself.

On each of the old tests I will say a few words: premising that in applying these and others to the text of the Elizabethan dramatists, two important issues are to be kept in view, viz., the chronological order of a series of plays ostensibly due to one author, and the discrimination of two or more distinct styles of composition in a single play traditionally attributed to one, two, or more authors. In the former case the tests are supplementary to the external evidences, while in the latter there are no external evidences at all.

I.—The final extra or redundant syllable test was first proposed by Roderick in his notes appended to Edwards' *Canons of Criticism*, and subsequently noticed by Malone in his essay entitled *An Attempt to ascertain the order in which the plays of Shakespeare were written.* 1st edition, January, 1778. In his remarks on *Henry VIII* he writes thus: "Mr. Roderick * * takes notice of some peculiarities in the metre of the play before us, viz., 'that there are more verses, in it, than in any other, which end with a redundant syllable—very near two to one—and that the cæsuræ or pauses of the verse are full as remarkable.' The *redundancy*, etc., observed by this critic, Mr. Steevens thinks 'was rather the effect of chance, than of design in the author; and might have arisen either from the negligence of Shakespeare * * * * or from the interpolations of Ben Jonson, whose hand Dr. Farmer thinks he occasionally perceives in the dialogue." Malone adds that the peculiarities in question favour the view that the play underwent alteration after it had left the hands of Shakespeare. The final redundant syllables in *Henry VIII* were first counted and tabulated by Mr. Spedding. A score of Shakespeare's plays were submitted to the same test by Professor Hertzberg, and Mr. Fleay has applied it to all the plays in the received collection, not excluding the doubtful ones; in fact to every extant play between 1580 and 1640.

II.—The stopt line test was first applied to Shakespeare's plays by the late Charles Bathurst. In his *Remarks on Shakespeare's Versification*, § 1, 1857, he writes—

His versification, in respect of the Cæsura, as it is called, or division of the pauses, differs most exceedingly [not merely] in different places, * * * * * * but generally, and in its extremes always between one play and another; *and it depends on the time of* his life. * * * * * * The great and primary point in which I conceive Shakespeare's versification altered, was the change from unbroken to interrupted verse. By interrupted verse, I do not mean so much that there is a pause or break in the middle [the Cæsura proper], as that you cannot dwell upon the end: and that, of course, may be true in different degrees. * * * * * * But the interruption of the verse was carried, in the latter part of his life, to an extreme, or rather he fell into another peculiarity, in making the verse end upon a perfectly weak monosyllable, such as *if* or *and*. [Light or weak ending.] This is capable of happening, where the verse itself is unbroken. Another change which certainly increased in the latter part of his life, on the whole, was the use of double endings;

and the author contrasts the versification of *The Tempest* with that of *The Comedy of Errors*, the former abounding in double endings, which we scarcely find in the latter. Mr. Furnivall in 1873 employed it for discriminating the double authorship of *Henry VIII.*

III.—The 'rhyme test' appears to have first engaged the attention of Edmund Malone. In his *Attempt to ascertain the order*, &c., 1778, he remarks on the abundance of rhymes in Shakespeare's early plays.

IV.—The 'middle cæsura test' was, as I have shewn, suggested by Bathurst.

V.—The 'light or weak ending test' was also suggested by Bathurst. Mr. Fleay has employed it to distinguish Massinger from Fletcher. It was first applied to Shakespeare by Professor Ingram, of Trinity College, Dublin, as a time-order test, and it serves in his hands to distinguish the fourth period of Shakespeare's work. His views are given in an extremely well written and accurate paper contributed to the *Transactions* of the New Shakspere Society for 1875. He has unfortunately brought this test into some discredit by pressing the difference of per-centages to an inadmissible extreme.

Of these five tests Mr. Fleay discards only the 'stopt line test.' In the sequent essay he employs the other four old tests, and all the new ones above enumerated. It will materially tend to the understanding both of processes and of results, if the reader, before proceeding to Mr. Fleay's essay, will take the trouble to study the tables, printed at the end of it, upon which that essay wholly depends.

III.

ON METRICAL TESTS APPLIED TO SHAKESPEARE.

BY F. G. FLEAY.

BEFORE entering into details it is necessary to answer the question, which of the metrical tests that have been proposed are applicable for the purpose of determining authorship or date of composition with especial reference to the plays of Shakespeare. It has been tacitly assumed, not only by critics who, not understanding the nature of these tests, or the psychological laws of which they are a consequence, have treated the whole question with ridicule, but also by sciolists, who, seeing that important results have been attained by their use, are desirous of ventilating their own names in connexion with them, that *any* linguistic peculiarity whatever can be used as a test. Mr. Swinburne, for instance, has wasted his splendid rhetoric on several occasions in satirizing an imaginary test-system based on such facts as this: 'A particular pronoun or conjunction is used in this play some fifty times oftener than it occurs in any other work of the author:' * and the literary organ of the New Shakspere Society announced some time ago the 'discovery' of a new metrical test called the broken-line-speech-ending, or something equivalent to that. Of course nothing comes of such discoveries, and only

* *Essay on G. Chapman's Poetical and Dramatic Works.* 1875. P. 50.

hindrance by such criticisms. If a chemist were to suggest that any acid whatever—say H_2SO_4, for instance—could be used as a universal test, he would simply be regarded as ignorant and presumptuous; and if any chemical essayist were to deny the possibility of chemical testimony on the ground that H_2SO_4 was not a discriminating class-test at all, he would be looked on as equally void of chemistry and logic. But the public have some interest in chemistry, in so far as they desire a means of detecting impure pickles or adulterated milk: in literary criticism they have no interest, except that the quarrels of those who should, beyond other men, support each other, are always amusing; hence they admit the sophistry in one case that in the other they would scorn.

In order to ascertain the tests that can be used for Shakespeare, we must examine the structure of his plays analytically. The first division of their contents is that into Prose and Verse. It has been proposed to make the amount of prose a test for chronological succession (time-order test): but this amount so clearly depends on the prominence given to prose-speaking characters in a play, and this again depends so much on the predominance of comic or tragic elements, that any general application of such a test would be absurd. Nevertheless it has some value: in some plays acknowledged to be partly only from the hand of Shakespeare, such as *Henry VIII*, *Pericles*, and *Timon*, the whole of the Shakespearian parts appear to be in verse. This to me indicates that these plays are not alterations of old plays made by Shakespeare (for in that case we should, I think, have found prose-scenes of his making): but rather alterations or completions of Shakespeare's work by other hands. Again, in *King John*, *Richard II*, *Richard III* (for i, 4 is corrupted verse), and *Edward III* we find no prose whatever; which indicates the strong predominance of the influence of Marlow, or of Marlow and Peele writing conjointly, in the earlier history-plays of Shakespeare. In his early Comedies he used prose abundantly from the very first: but did not introduce the comic element into his Histories (though he did into his one early tragedy, *Romeo and Juliet*) till 1 *Henry IV* (date 1597). It is necessary, then, that with these exceptions (which are brought out in the Prose column of our tables in the Appendix) we should confine ourselves to the Verse parts for time-testing.

The main division of the verse parts is certainly that into its rhyming and rhymeless or blank lines. The normal line is, of course, one of five feet or measures or beats, whether rhymed or rhymeless, such as—

He needs | no in | direct | or law | less course.

The main bulk of the plays (except the very earliest) is formed of such lines without rhyme, and the gradual diminution of the proportion between the rhyme and blank lines is maintained by me to be one of the chief time-tests that we can apply: to ascertain these proportions it is necessary to tabulate the blank lines (as in the 'blank' column in the tables) and the rhymed lines. But there is not only a gradual lessening, as we advance in time, of rhyme lines in general: but also a gradual dying-out of different arrangements of rhyme lines: Heroic couplets do not absolutely disappear till the very last: even in *The Tempest* (1610-11) we find—

> Prospero my lord shall know what I have done:
> So, King, go safely on to meet thy son.

But lines alternately rhyming do not continue nearly so long: their last appearance is probably in *As You Like It* (*c.* 1598-9).

> Hang there, my verse, in witness of my love:
>   And thou, thrice-crowned queen of night, survey
> With thy chaste eye from thy pale sphere above
>   Thy huntress' name, that my full life doth sway.

Similar lines occur in every play (except *Richard III*, which I believe for many reasons to be founded on an earlier non-Shakespearean play) up to 1598, and the first play in which they do not occur is 2 *Henry IV*. I should notice that the alternate rhymes in *All's Well that Ends Well* are probably of the early sketch, that play having been re-written *c.* 1601 from a very early one. Such lines, then, form an important period test, and I have therefore tabulated them in the column headed 'Alternate.' It was not necessary to put 'Sonnets' (which are in Shakespeare only three quatrains of alternates plus a rhyming couplet) in a separate column for test purposes: but as the occurrence of Sonnets in the plays is important as bearing on the date of production of the Sonnets published in 1609, it may be noted that such Sonnets occur in *Love's Labour Lost*, *All's Well That Ends Well*, *Romeo and Juliet* (Prologue and Chorus) and *Henry V* (Epilogue). This last Epilogue is of doubtful authorship: the date of the revised *Romeo and Juliet* is 1596-7, which I believe to be the limit of Shakespeare's sonnet writing, though if the Epilogue to *Henry V* be his, he wrote one in 1599. Again, it is only in the early plays that we find doggrel lines of uncertain number in their syllables, and varying from four to six measures or beats. These occur for the last time in the *Merchant of Venice* (*c.* 1595).

> Come, Nerissa. Sirrah, go before.
> Whiles we shut the gates upon one wooer, another knocks at the door.

These again are important as a test for the early comedies giving us this order: *Love's Labour's Lost* (first draft), *Comedy of Errors, Two Gentlemen of Verona, Merchant of Venice.* If there were any in the first draft of *Midsummer Night's Dream* (as there may well have been), they must have been carefully expunged in the revision of that play in 1600.

Besides the afore-named rhyme lines we have still left a number of short lines, mostly four-measure trochaics, such as

> Pay with falsehood false exacting,
> And perform an old contracting.

These and the songs of various measures from which they can only be separated by being meant for speech, not for singing, are of no use as tests, but are tabulated for completeness' sake.

We now come to the blank lines: these are chiefly of five-measures, but some are of one, *e. g.*:

> Swear!
> Nay then!
> Ay, master!

Some of two:

Who | comes here?
Fleance | is scaped.
One might | interpret.

Some of three:

This | is kind | I offer.
Leaving | no track | behind.
Else sure | ly his | had e | qualled.

Some of six:

How dares | thy harsh | rude tongue ‖ sound this | unplea | sing news?

The only value of the two and three measure lines as tests is to confirm the early production of the first period plays in which they very rarely occur: it is necessary, however, to tabulate these, if only to shew their uncertain occurrence and to point out the reason of it. Many of these plays were revised, rewritten, abridged, and otherwise altered; sometimes by Shakespeare himself, and occasionally (after his death) by others: in cutting out or inserting passages no regard whatever was had to the metre at the beginning of the alterations, and little at the end. Hence the introduction of broken or short lines to an extent that the writer did not originally contemplate. For example: *Hamlet*, I, iv, 17—38, was omitted in the abridged Folio acting copy: this passage ends

To his own scandal . . .

In the Folio therefore,

. . . Look, my lord, it comes!

stands as an imperfect line.

In *Lear* iii, i, 30—42, is a passage that was inserted for a Court representation of the play: this ends with

This office to you.

Which accordingly stands as a broken line in the Quarto. These instances must here suffice: I have treated fully of this question in an article forthcoming in the *Epitome of Literature* (Philadelphia).*

The one-measure lines can hardly be separated from the six-measure, as it is very hard indeed to say why

Come, come, you'll never meet a more sufficient man—*Othello*, iii, 4. 90,

should be *two* lines: but

Will you take eggs for money?
No, my lord!
I'll fight. *Winter's Tale*, I, ii, 161.

should be *one* line. Yet that is the arrangement of Messrs. Clark and Wright. I have, therefore, thought it desirable to discuss the six-measure lines fully in minute detail further on: and to omit their separate tabulation for reasons hereafter given. Four-measure lines such as

And there | repose | you for | this night.

are mere corruptions arising from a word being dropt in writing or printing: there are very few of them in Shakespeare. But such lines as

On your | command. || I know't | too well.
Hark, Hark. || I hear | the mins | trels play,

* Written in September, 1879; but now in March, 1880, the Epitome has been dead five months, and the proposed paper remains in MS.

are really not single but compound lines of 2 + 2 beats and 1 + 3 beats respectively. Lines of the former kind are often useful as tests, not of time of production but of the printers' reliability: and those of the latter frequently indicate that a passage has been omitted for stage purposes.

We may, then, now arrange our analysis of the lines in a play thus:

Prose.				
Verse.	Rhyme.	Five-measure.	Heroic.	1
			Alternate.	2
			Sonnet.	
		Short-line.	Dialogue.	
			Song.	
		Doggrel.		3
	Blank.	Five-measure.		
		Two ,,		
		Three ,,		4
		Four ,,		
		One ,,		5
		Six ,,		

and on this analysis base the following tests:

1.—The Rhyme test for determining succession of the plays generally: I do this, not by taking the absolute amount of rhyme, but by taking the ratio of the number of rhyme lines in the verse scenes to the total number of lines in the verse scenes; and the result is in all cases consistent with the dates given in [ ] at the head of each table in the Appendix, and so are the results of all other tests that I have used.

2.—The Alternate Line test, for determining the order of the First and Second Period plays, *i.e.*, up to 1598 inclusive.

3.—The Doggrel test, for the earliest plays only.

4.—The Short Line blank test (with four-measure line test when the measures break into 2 + 2, 1 + 3, 3 + 1), for determining where passages have been omitted, or rather for confirming æsthetic conclusions on this matter.

5.—The Alexandrine test, specially for determining the order of the later plays.

But besides the tests founded on this total analysis of a play's metre, there are others founded on the construction of five and six-measure lines taken individually. Thus we have

6.—The Female (or double or extra syllable) ending of such lines as

And yet | partake | no ven | om for | his know | *ledge.*

This test was incompletely and inaccurately worked out by Herzberg simultaneously with me. His errors seem to me to arise partly from confusing such lines as

Of stuft | suffic | iency | : now from | the o | racle,

which is merely a female-ending line with two extra syllables, with a true Alexandrine, such as

As is | a dead | man's nose. || Yet I | do see't | and feel't. ||

and partly from using some emended or improperly arranged text. It is necessary for true tabulation that no line should be counted an Alexandrine unless the second syllable of the last measure be accented; and that the lines be properly divided on

Shakespeare's scheme of rhythm, not in the hap-hazard way of certain popular editions which I forbear to name.

7.—The Mid-line (female or double or) Extra syllable, in such lines as

> Haled out | to mur | *der* : || my-self | on ev- | ery post.

These lines are now tabulated for the first time in the 'Extra middle syllable' column, the term 'female' being kept for the preceding test. This test is chiefly useful for determing proximity to the change from the Second to the Third Period: the greatest number of such lines are found in *Measure for Measure* (1603).

8.—I thought at one time that the number of 'tag-rhymes' spoken by an actor at the end of a scene or on leaving the stage or at the end of an important speech might help us: but the rhyme-test in its usual shape gives more reliable results.

I must mention here a point that is important, and I believe new. Allowance must be made, where the results of several tests are compared, for their mutual interference. For example:

1.—Female endings and unstopt lines in a metrically good author do not certainly advance *pari passu*. Such lines as

> Doublets, I think, flew up: and had their *faces*
> Been loose, &c.

are only defensible on the ground that *faces* was pronounced *face'*: a slight pause is needed after a female ending.

2.—Rhymes and female endings are almost incompatible owing to the paucity of rhyming paroxyton words.

3.—Rhymes and weak endings are incompatible, emphatic syllables being necessary in the rhyming words.

4.—Scarce any weak endings are female, hence the introduction of weak endings must (and does, see table) interfere with the progressive number of female endings. Similar remarks apply in other cases too numerous even to enumerate here. Other linguistic tests, not metrical—such as the ἅπαξ λεγόμενα test and others that I have worked out elsewhere do not come within the plan of this essay: nor do tests that I have applied to authors other than Shakespeare; such as the weak-ending test for Massinger and the elided-v test for Chapman, the trisyllabic-foot test for Peele, and so on. For any peculiarity to be a test at all it must be one that distinctly varies in considerable degree at different periods of an author's life or in the usage of different authors: and it must be capable of accurate numeration. I have not found that any tests except those which I have used fulfil these two canons.

I now proceed, in accordance with Dr. Ingleby's request, to state concisely the general results of my investigations on this test question.

I must first of all state on what amount of research my results are based. I have examined, counted, and tabulated the works of Greene, Peele, Marlow, Shakespeare, Chapman, Jonson, Dekker, Heywood, Middleton, Marston, Webster, Beaumont, Fletcher, Tourneur, Rowley, Massinger, Ford, Shirley, Randolph, Brome, Glapthorne, Suckling, Davenant, Dryden, Lee, Tennyson, and Byron; the plays in Hazlitt's *Dodsley*, the Shakespeare Society's publications, and Simpson's

School of Shakespeare: besides such unreprinted plays as I could get access to in original editions. For all these I have noted the following tests: 1. Rhymes. 2. Female endings. 3. Short lines. 4. Alexandrines. For most of them I have marked but not tabulated the weak-endings; and for nearly every author I have noted some specific or characteristic peculiarity which serves to distinguish him from others. The following are among the general results I have obtained:

1.—When two authors wrote a play in conjunction it is always possible to separate their work as long as they did not revise each others' writings: the only instance I have found where the work cannot be absolutely separated is that of certain plays in which Beaumont's *comic* writing has been revised by Fletcher, and this is a matter of rare occurrence. Beaumont's *tragic* scenes can always be distinguished.

2.—On the other hand, when a play has been written over, and the lines touched up for revisal (I do not mean patched by insertion of long passages), it is not possible to separate the work, although it is always easy to see where this process has been going on. Many of Fletcher's plays were treated in this way by Shirley.

3.—It is not so easy in some cases to affix the authorship of an anonymous play as it is to separate a play between various authors. Generally, however, if the date of production can be ascertained the difficulty is much lightened. Every author writes differently at different periods of his life, and it is not uncommon for the plays of a dramatist in his early career to be metrically more like to those of some contemporary than to those of the same author at a later stage. Heywood gives us a striking instance of this, which I shall have to recur to.

4.—In order to obtain accurate results in determining authorship it is absolutely necessary that we should have several works of the author entirely genuine and authentic from which to select our tests. Otherwise the grossest errors may result. As a salient instance I may mention statements put forth in various papers of the New Shakspere Society with regard to theories of mine, *e. g.*, that I have wrongly assigned trisyllabic feet to Peele rather than to Greene, and the like. The conclusions arrived at by the authors of these papers are based on erroneous data. They assume Peele's authorship of *Clyamon* and *Clamydes* on Dyce's verdict: they take Greene's *Orlando* into their metrical data—a mutilated adulterated version, of which scarcely any portion remains as Greene wrote it: they are ignorant of the fact that several plays passing under single names of these writers were undoubtedly written by them in conjunction: all this vitiates their premises and renders their conclusions futile.

5.—On the whole then we may say that by means of metrical tests we can always distinguish, generally determine authorship: we can also usually ascertain at what period of an author's life a work was written: for authors often adopt peculiarities or drop them quite suddenly. It is certain, for instance, that *Othello* and *Hamlet* belong to one period of Shakespeare's work, and that *Romeo* and *Coriolanus* do not. But the abuse of this principle cannot be too carefully guarded against. The notion that the order of percentage, say of weak-endings or of female-endings, must coincide with the time-order of production, is fallacious. It is here that I differ from all others who have examined this subject. Hertzberg and Ingram, for instance, have tried to assign a definite chronological order based on minute percentages of metrical peculiarities, and have demonstrably failed. The conclusions drawn by me as to authorship or date are always based on large numerical differences; in fact a series of gradual increment in any metrical characteristic in chronological sequence would be opposed to my theory that such characteristics are for the most part suddenly adopted or resigned. Against this exact percentage-differential doctrine Mr. Swinburne's arguments are conclusive; and it is to be regretted that it should have been adopted by so eminent a critic as Professor Ingram; inasmuch as it tends to cast ridicule on the sounder views which have led me to the determination of many disputed questions, as will be seen in my forthcoming treatise on the Drama of 1550 to 1650, its Authors, Companies, Theatres, and Actors.

6.—To this doctrine, however, there is one important exception: the percentage-rhyme-test. This test is for the period 1590-1640, much more closely in accordance with chronology than any other. And there is good reason for its being so. From the time when Marlow, in opposition to Greene, introduced blank verse, until the decadence of the stage in 1642, there was in all other metrical matters continual oscillation. The unstopt lines, with many weak-endings, of Massinger's in 1620-40, had their prototype in Shakespeare's of 1606-12; the numerous female endings of Shirley's, 1625-40, and

Ford's, 1621–40. were transmitted from Fletcher, 1610–24. The mixture of prose and verse in Shirley was taken from Greene, Peele, and Shakespeare; yet Marlow, Fletcher, and Massinger never adopted it. In all these matters each man did as he liked—some used prose, some blank, some frequent short lines, some none at all: some weak-endings, some trisyllabic feet, some female endings, some Alexandrines; but none of these things were patent to the public. Then, as now, people liked or disliked the ring of Marlow or Fletcher, or Jonson, as they do of Browning, Tennyson, or Swinburne, but they do not notice the technical differences between them. But as to the use of rhyme, the question is different. Not only is there a gradual disuse of rhyme by every author* of the period in question as he grows older, but there was also a growing dislike on the part of the public to the mixture of rhyme and blank in stage plays. I must give some evidence on this matter, as it is altogether ignored by such writers as Professor Dowden, whose Shakespeare Primer is unfortunately crowded with inaccuracies on this and kindred subjects. In the Epilogue to Heywood's *Royal King and Loyal Subject*, as published in 1637, and acted *c.* 1603, he says:

> We know (and not long since) there was a time
> Strong lines were not looked after; but if rime,
> O then 'twas excellent.
> And what's now out of fashion who can tell
> But it may come in fashion and suit well?

* Dr. B. Nicholson alleged the contrary of Jonson, and used the statement against me. His allegation is altogether contrary to the facts.

Note that this play was originally written some thirty years before it was published, and that the text bears internal evidence to its original form as a rhyme-play. This shews most strongly in act iv, scene 3, in which there are still left some two dozen rhymes, but the whole scene was originally rhyme, and can be easily restored in many places. Heywood has merely altered rhyme-words, or made transpositions to suit the altered taste of the public. I give instances with my supposed original form of the lines in [ ], and the later alterations in italics.

You are our sister, and that royal *title* [name]
From all disgrace your freedom shall proclaim.
His bounty we will equal and *exceed* [excell]:
W'have power to better what in him's not well.
I should avow she not *the Queen alone* [alone the Queen]
Excells in grace, but all that I have seen.
How say you, Lords? have we requited *well* [yet]
Our subject's bounty? are we in his debt?
Your highness is in courtesy *invincible* [alone],
And bountiful beyond comparison.
No, sir, thank you; your master yet will yield,
And leave to us the honour of the *day* [field.]
I fear our fate: if once the Marshal rise,
Down, down, must we. Therefore *devise some plot* [some plot devise].
What have we here? A jewel I should rate
Were it my own, above your crown and *sceptre* [state]
A child! a prince! *one of your royal blood* [of your blood-royal one]
Behold him, King, my grandchild and thy son;
Your vassal and your servant that have strove,
Only to give you and your royal *princess* [love].
Not to requite, &c.
But shall I give't o'er thus? 'tis in my *head* [brain]
How I this lost day's honour shall regain.
A gift as great, as rich, *have I in store* [in store have I].

With which *to gratify our subject's love* [our subject's love to gratify];
Thou'st given me a grandchild and *a son* [an heir],
A royal infant, and to me most dear.
Your father, son, and subject quite surpast,
Yields himself vanquisht and o'ercome at *length* [last].
He that the father doth so much respect,
Shouldn't, methinks, the daughter's love *despise* [reject].

There can be, I think, no doubt that the above scene was written in rhyme; in judging on this point, however, if the reader has not the play to turn to he should be informed that these lines occur imbedded in the midst of others that do rhyme in the play as it has come down to us. We can hardly suppose this to have been an isolated instance, or Heywood to have been singular in this practice. It is then, I think, a fair hypothesis to start from, that the growing tendency of the times in favour of blank verse, combined with the natural inclination of each individual poet to abandon rhyme more and more as he got older, would produce in the chronological series of his writing a greater regularity of decrease than could be paralleled from any other of the metrical tests. And this I have found to be true in *every* case where the dates of an author's plays can be definitely ascertained. Jonson and Ford are salient instances. The hypothesis is also confirmed by the general literary history of modern nations. Alliteration, anapæstic movements, preference of melodious sound to weighty thoughtful sense, are the marks of youthful poets, undeveloped nations, decadent periods of literature: the greatest men who mark the high tides of poetic art always culminate in a rhythm so delicate, so free from these juvenile tricks and artifices, that to the untrained ear it seems to border on prose. Dr. Johnson could not appreciate Milton's blank verse: the contemporaries of Dryden preferred his rhymes to Shakespeare's finest passages of rhymeless music; but the tendency of progressive training and culture is in the direction I have stated for the individual as well as for the nation.

But this law is apparently greatly interfered with whenever, as in the case of Heywood's plays above cited, revision, either by the author himself or some other hand, has been made for revival performances. And I confidently state that more than half the plays that have come down to us from the Shakespeare time have been so altered. Hence it is impossible to draw up lists for rhyme, like Hertzberg's for female endings, which shall have any value if taken alone. In Shakespeare's plays especially it is necessary to take into account the alterations made at different periods; many of his plays have demonstrably been altered twice at least, and the disputes as to the date of a play's production which do not take this into account are meaningless and absurd. For instance, some say *The Merry Wives* was written in 1592, some in 1598, some in 1604. All are partly right; and all wrong in excluding the other hypotheses. Shakespeare (perhaps in conjunction with some one else) wrote a play in 1592, which was revived with alterations in 1598–9, and finally altered as we have it in 1604; but our present play is neither of 1592, nor of 1598, nor of 1604, but of all three. I have stated my views on this matter at the head of each of the tables of Shakespeare's plays printed in this volume, in the Appendix at the end of this chapter.

For general chronological arrangement, then, I attach the

highest importance to this rhyme test. For separating the periods of Shakespeare's work, I rank the weak-ending test first in distinguishing the third and fourth periods: the extra middle syllable for separating the second and third: the rhyme test for separating the first and second. For determining where revision has been at work the short lines, especially at the beginning and end of speeches, are most useful. The Alexandrine test I have examined at length further on. Of course it is not necessary here to treat of the use of tests in distinguishing Shakespearian authorship, as I have already stated my views concerning most of Shakespeare's plays elsewhere. I will merely say that in many instances of which I hope to give the result in my forthcoming book, I have obtained satisfactory conclusions, and confirmed them by evidence of an entirely different nature. There is still one Shakespearian problem only partially solved, namely, the authorship of 2, 3, *Henry VI*: but the unsolved question is really this: what share had Marlow, Greene, and Peele, respectively, in the matter? That Shakespeare had *none* I have stated elsewhere; and I have now additional evidence in confirmation of this view. I notice the point here because it seems that the tests break down: they do not; what really breaks down is the generally received evidence as to the authorship (in entirety) of *Orlando*, the *Battle of Alcazar*, &c., and without these points settled we are powerless for want of a basis from which to conduct operations.

I have given below, besides the full treatment of Shakespeare's Alexandrines, tables of all the tests I have applied to his plays for each act and scene, nearly as these tables were prepared for the

New Shakspere Society in 1874: the statement in the transactions of that Society that I had not prepared them in this shape is not correct, as my correspondence with the Director distinctly shews. In the tables as now printed, I have, however, made some alterations. I have thrown the Alexandrines into the total of blank lines: it is very difficult to distinguish trisyllabic endings from Alexandrines; and with the full separate treatment of Alexandrines here given no practical benefit is gained by tabulating them separately: a large number of accidental rhymes is omitted; this is certainly an improvement: an additional column (of extra middle syllables) is added: and the tables are so arranged as to admit of being checked by adding horizontally and vertically. I have thus detected several errors in my previously printed tables. Without such checks it is not easy for an isolated worker to avoid errors, though it is easy for esthetic compilers to crow over every misprint or slip of the pen they can detect in the books which they use as the source of their own compilations.

I have finally to point out that unless we have perfectly accurate and authentic texts, such tests as weak-endings and Alexandrines cannot be applied on the percentage system. A division of the lines differing from the received one will often introduce or remove instances of these: and when no line-division, or an absurdly incorrect one, exists in the original editions, we are at the mercy of editors who do not tell us of their alterations. Dyce, for instance, had not ear enough to know whether a line was deficient or not, Gifford alters his text to suit his notions of metre. Stevens introduced emendations *ad libitum*, Clarke and Wright have mistaken Fletcher's verse (in

Henry VIII) for prose, and the vagaries of German editors in metrical matters completely destroy any possibility of using their texts for any purpose but popular editions. The only tests that can be tabulated with numerical certainty are the rhyme tests and the extra syllable tests, whether at the end or in the middle of a line. The so-called stopt-line test will of course discriminate the date of the *Comedy of Errors* from that of *Winter's Tale:* but its author was never silly enough to use it on the percentage system, and his followers (or follower) have taken care not to try its merit by counting a dozen plays of dates approximately known.

Before passing to the detailed consideration of the Alexandrine test for Shakespeare, I will merely enumerate some of the *certain* conclusions of my metrical investigations by way of sample. Of course I cannot here give detailed proofs, but these will appear in my forthcoming work above referred to.

1.—Chapman did not write *Revenge for Honour* or *Alphonsus Emperor of Germany.*

2.—Marston wrote part only of *The Insatiate Countess.*

3.—Heywood wrote part of *Hoffmann.*

4.—Chettle and Haughton wrote *Grim the Collier of Croydon.*

5.—Heywood (not J. Cooke) wrote *How a Man may choose a Good Wife from a bad.*

6.—Marlow wrote only the following scenes in *Faustus:* i 1, 3, ii 1, 2 (part), iii 1 (part), 2 (part), v 3, 4 (part), as they occur in the 1604 Quarto. [Scenes 1, 3, 5, 6, 14, 15, 16.]*

* This statement is fully confirmed by Wagner's independent investigations published since I sent the MS. of this chapter to Dr. Ingleby.

For discriminations of joint authorship in plays, I must refer to my forthcoming treatise.

THE ALEXANDRINE TEST.

In *Love's Labour's Lost* Alexandrines occur in ii 1, 135, iii 1, 176, v 2, 47, 261. It is doubtful whether the third of these should stand: we might read,

But what was sent to you from fair Dumain?

omitting 'Katherine:' names of persons addrest are frequently inserted in the text from the prompter's marginal directions. The fourth is remarkable as shewing the early use by Shakespeare of Spenserian Alexandrines without cesura after the third foot.

Fleeter than arrows, bullets, wind, thought, swifter things.

In *Midsummer's Night's Dream* there are none.

In the *Comedy of Errors* they occur ii 2, 120, iii 1, 1, iv 1, 21 (a very questionable line), 41, iv 4, 16, 139, v 1, 174, 208. Of these the following are worthy of notice:

No: bear it with you | lest I come not time enough. iv 1, 41.

To a ropes end, sir: | and to that end am I returned. iv 4, 16.

He did be-speak a chain for me: | but had it not. iv 4, 139.

His master preaches patience to him, | and the while. v 1, 174.

To-day did dine together: | so befall my soul
As this is false he burdens me withal. v 1, 208.

Some of these lines are so unlike Shakespeare's usual early metrical work that I regard them as open to emendation. I cannot however enter on that question in this place.

The Alexandrines in *Richard II* are so numerous and exceptional as to require special treatment: I have therefore extracted them in full.

(1) i 1, 204. Lord marshal, command | our officers at arms.
(2) i 3, 83. Rouse up thy youthful blood: | be valiant and live.
(3) ii 1, 141. (I do) beseech your majesty | impute his words.
(4) ii 1, 94. Ill in myself to see, | and in thee seeing ill.
(5) ii 1, 250. As blanks, benevolences, | and I wot not what.
(6) ii 1, 254. That which | his noble ancestors achieved with blows.
(7) ii 2, 24. More than your lord's departure weep not; | more's not seen.
(8) ii 2, 29. Persuades me it is otherwise: | howe'er it be.
(9) ii 2, 90. Sirrah, | get thee to Plashy, to my sister Gloster.
(10) ii 2, 53. The Lord Northumberland, | his son young Henry Percy.
(11) ii 2, 87. The nobles they are fled, | the commons they are cold.
(12) ii 2, 103. What, | are there no posts despatch'd for I'reland?
(13) ii 2, 111. If I know | how, or which way, to order these affairs.
(14) i 3, 123. Draw near, | and list, what with our council we have done.
(15) i 4, 11. Farewell: | and for my heart disdainèd that my tongue.
(16) i 4, 65. Amen.
(17) ii 3, 29. He was not so resolved | when last we spake together.
(18) ii 3, 55. And in it are the Lords | of York, Berkley, and Seymour.
(19) ii 3, 120. A wandering vagabond; | my rights and royalties.
(20) ii 3, 168. It may be I will go with you: | but yet I'll pause.
(21) ii 1, 258. Reproach and dissolution | hangeth over him.
(22) i 1, 12. As near as I could sift him | on that argument.
(23) ii 4, 6. The king | reposeth all his confidence in thee.
(24) iii 1, 2. A happy gentleman | in blood and lineaments.
(25) iii 1, 29. Condemns you to the death. | See them deliver'd over.
(26) iii 2, 3. After your late tossing on the breaking seas.
(27) iii 2, 90. Hath power enough to serve our turn: | but who comes here?

(28) iii 3, 30. O | belike it is the bishop of Carlisle.
(29) iii 3, 27. And with him are the lord Aumerle, | lord Salisbury.
(30) iii 3, 45. The which | how far off from the mind of Bolingbroke.
(31) iii 3, 70. Controlling majesty: | alack, alack for woe.
(32) iii 5, 122. And as I am a gentleman | I credit him.
(33) iii 4, 73. Thou | old Adam's likeness, set to dress this garden.
(34) iii 4, 74. How dares thy harsh rude tongue | sound this unpleasing news?
(35) iv 1, 89. To all his lands and seignories: | when he's return'd.
(36) iv 1, 126. And he himself not present. | O forfend it, God.
(37) iv 1, 171. Found truth in all but one: | I, in twelve thousand, none.
(38) iv 1, 326. My lord: | before I freely speak my mind herein.
(39) iv 1, 329. To bury mine intents, | but also to effect.
(40) v 2, 28. Did scowl on gentle Richard: no man cried | God save him.
(41) v 2, 65. 'Tis nothing but some bond | that he is enter'd into.
(42) v 2, 70. (I do) beseech you, pardon me; | I may not show it.
(43) v 2, 86. Give me my boots, I say. | Why, York, what wilt thou do?
(44) v 2, 101. Away, fond woman: | were he twenty times my son.
(45) v 2, 117. Till Bolingbroke | have pardon'd thee: | Away, begone.
(46) v 3, 24. What means our cousin, that he stares and looks | so wildly?
(47) v 3, 25. God save your grace. | I do beseech your majesty.
(48) v 3, 39. Have thy desire: | my liege, beware: | look to thyself.
(49) v 3, 42. Stay thy revengeful hand: | thou hast no cause to fear.
(50) v 3, 101. His eyes do drop no tears: | his prayers are in jest.
(51) v 4, 2. Have I | no friend will rid me of this living fear?
(52) v 4, 52. Their watches on unto my eyes, | the outward watch.
(53) v 5, 75. To look | upon my sometime royal master's face.
(54) v 5, 110. That staggers thus my person. | Exton, thy fierce hand.

It is absolutely certain that in no unadulterated play anterior to *Measure for Measure*, and only in one of those surreptitiously published, viz., *Romeo and Juliet*, does even half the number of Alexandrines occur that we meet with here. I cannot believe that Shakespeare adopted the use of them in this one play only during thirteen years, a period comprising two-thirds of his dramatic career, and moreover did it very badly: many of the lines in the above list are most unsatisfactory to the ear. I, therefore, would rather see in this peculiarity a proof of incorrect printing or carelessness in revising the original 1593 copy for the press in 1597, than a sudden alteration of style hastily adopted and as hastily abandoned. This view is confirmed by the fact that the first quartos of *Romeo and Juliet* and of this play were the very first of Shakespeare's dramas that were printed: and consequently it is in them, if in any, that we must expect such inaccuracies. A large number of these Alexandrines demand pitiless correction: those in *Romeo and Juliet* had it, no doubt, from Shakespeare's own hand in 1598, Q 2, only one year after the issue of Q 1. Why *Richard II* was left uncorrected we have no means of ascertaining.

In No. 3 then omit 'I do:' in No. 5 read 'benevolence'' (plural): in No. 6 omit 'noble' (as in F): in No. 7 omit 'your lord's,' which words are repeated from a line above: in No. 8 omit 'it is:' and in No. 9 either put 'Sirrah' in a line by itself or omit 'Gloster:' in No. 12 either put 'what' in a separate line or omit 'no:' No. 13 arrange thus:

> Gent'men, will you go muster men? If *I* know
> How or which way, &c.

In No. 14 put 'Draw near' in a separate line: in No. 15 treat 'Farewell' in the same way: and so 'Amen' in No. 16: in No. 20 read 'May be I'll go with you, but yet I'll pause:' in No.

21 read 'o'er him:' No. 22 is a trisyllabic ending, not an Alexandrine: in No. 23 the repetition of 'the king' in two consecutive lines looks corrupt; I suspect, however, that 'reposeth' should be 'rests' or 'puts:' In No. 26 'after' is one syllable (this is unusual): In No. 27 omit 'enough:' in No. 28 put 'O' in a separate line: in No. 29 'Sal'sb'ry' is two syllables: in No. 30 put 'the which' in a separate line: No. 32 is a trisyllabic ending: and No. 33 arrange

O, I am prest to death,
Through want of speaking. [*Pause.*] Thou,
Old Adam's likeness, &c.

In No. 35 read 'And tho' mine enemy restored to all | His lands,' &c., omitting 'again.' In No. 36 omit 'And he:' in No. 38 put 'my lord' in a separate line: in No. 40 put 'God save him' in a separate line: in No. 42 omit 'I do' as in No. 3: in No. 44 arrange

Away, fond woman: were he twenty times
My son, I would appeach him.
Hadst thou groan'd
For him, as I have done, thou'ldst be more pitiful.

In No. 45 omit 'Away' or 'begone:' in No. 46 arrange

But who comes here?
Where is the king?
What means
Our cousin, that he stares and looks so wildly?

In No. 47 pronounce 'mai'esty:' in No. 48 punctuate

Have thy desire. My liege! | Beware; look to thyself!

No. 51 is perhaps a case of Spenserian Alexandrine with

hephthememeral cesura: No. 52 is another with cesura after the fourth foot: in No. 53 I would omit 'at length,' and read

> With much ado have gotten leave to look
> Upon my sometime royal master's face.

In No. 54 I would omit 'Exton,' the vocative of the person addressed, which is so often inserted from stage directions. Be it, however, clearly understood: that I would not (except in re-arranging some few divisions of lines) on any account interfere with the received text editorially by inserting emendations on these hypothetical grounds: I am merely pointing out probable cures for the numerous printer's or copyist's errrors by which the text of this play has got into its present condition: so as to remove the palpable discrepancy which it presents from all other plays in this metrical matter of Alexandrines. That there are gross corruptions of metre in it is also clear from the number of lines of four feet which I have not space to enter on here: and from the parallel case of *Romeo and Juliet*, where the Alexandrines *have been corrected by Shakespeare* in the same way as I have tried to correct those of *Richard II.* These we now proceed to consider (the lines are numbered as in Daniel's edition).

(1) 1, 3, 33. He was a merry man. Dost thou fall forward, Juliet?

'Juliet' (vocative) should be omitted. It does not occur in Q 2.

(2) 1, 4, 48. But 'tis no wit to go. Why, Romeo, may one ask?

'Romeo' (vocative) omitted rightly in Q 2.

(3) 1, 5, 87. Peace, peace, thou talk'st of nothing. True, I talk of dreams.

By comparison with Q 2 we get the true reading.

> This is she.
> Peace, Mercutio, peace, peace.
> Thou talk'st of nothing.
> True, I talk of dreams.

(4) 1, 5, 31. How long is it since you and I were in a mask?

See Q 2, where this passage is correctly given.

(5) 4, 2, 167. With repetition of my Romeo's name.
Romeo! It is my soul that calls upon my name.

In Q 2. 'With repetition of my Romeo. | It is,' &c., rightly. 'Romeo' was a marginal correction for 'Romeo's name:' the printer has kept both the correction and the word to be corrected. Prosaic editors still keep the old reading which Shakespeare rejected.

(6) 4, 2, 177. Romeo, I have forgot why I do call thee back.

Another vocative (Romeo) rightly cut out in Q 2.

(7) 3, 1, 53. Marry, go before into the field, and he may be your follower.

In Q 2. 'Marry, go before to field, he'll be your follower.'

(8) 3, 1, 197. Mercy to all but murd'rers, pardoning none that kill.

In Q 2. 'Mercy but murders, pardoning those that kill.'

(9) 3, 2, 88. There is no truth, no faith, no honesty in men.

Still worse in Q 2 (which refer to '). My reading published some time since is—

> There's no trust,
> No faith, no honesty in men: all naught,
> All perjured, all dissemblers, all forsworn.

(10) 3. 3. 21. And world-exiled is death, calling death banishment.

A line dropt from the similarity of the endings of the two lines. In Q 2 rightly:

> And world's exile is death. Then banishèd
> Is death misterm'd. Calling death banishèd,

(11) 3. 3. 153. Ascend her chamber window: hence, and comfort her.

Q 2 omits 'window' rightly. Note this.

(12, 13) 3. 4. 12. Sir Paris? I'll make a desperate tender of my child.
I think she will be ruled in all respects by me.

Rightly in Q 2:

> Sir Paris, I will make a desperate tender
> Of my child's love. I think she will be ruled
> In all respects by me.

(14) iii 4. 24. We'll make no great ado: a friend or two, or so:

Q 2 omits 'or so' rightly.

(15) iii 4. 28. And make no more ado. | But what say you to Thursday?

Q 2 'And there an end. But what say you to Thursday?' Rightly. 'Ado' is repeated from l. 24.

(16) iii 4. 32. Wife, go you to your daughter ere you go to bed.

Q 2, rightly, 'Go you to Juliet ere,' &c.

(17) iii 5. 7. And not the nightingale. See, love, what envious streaks

Q 2 'No nightingale. Look, love,' &c.

(18) iii 5. 40. Your mother's coming to your chamber. Make all sure.

Q 2 omits 'Make all sure,' and reads 'Your lady mother,' &c.

(19) iii 5. 143. What says she to't? I have. But she will none. She thanks ye.

Q 2: 'Ay, sir, but she will none. She give[s] you thanks.'

(20) iii 5, 185. For here we need it not. My lord, ye are too hot.

Q 2 omits 'My lord.'

(21) iii 5, 185. God's blessed mother, wife, it mads me day, night, early, late.

My emendation to this passage has been published in Mr. Daniel's edition.

(22) iii 5, 208. I do beseech you, madam, cast me not away.

Q 2: 'O sweet my mother cast me not away,' &c. Compare 'I do beseech you' (twice) in *Richard II.* Cf. above; pp. 72, 73.

(23) iii 5, 243. And to be absolved. I will, and this is wisely done.

Corrected in Q 2, which see.

(24) v 1, 55. Did but forerun my need: and hereabout he dwells.

This passage is vilely given in Q 1, evidently not from an authentic copy. Right in Q 2. The same remark holds for

(25) v 1, 86. Than this which thou hast given me. Go, hie thee hence.

(26) v 3, 50. That murder'd my love's corse. ʌ I will apprehend him.

This passage is authentic in Q 1, but three lines have been omitted at ʌ for stage purposes. There is no Alexandrine in the full text.

(27) v 3, 314. Come, let us hence to have more talk of these sad things.

Q 2 reads 'Go hence' rightly. I 2, 52, 1 5, 40, might also be stretched into Alexandrines, thus making 29 in all (misprinted 92 in my *Shakespeare Manual*), but I think that only twenty-seven can be properly admitted: and *every one* of these is corrected in the revised Q 2. Surely the Alexandrines in *Richard II* stand in the same predicament. They are printers' or editors' verse, not Shakespeare's. The Alexandrines in *Romeo and Juliet*, Q 2, are i 2, 2, Globe edition (not in Q 1): Pope omits 'I think' i 3, 47, where Q 1 leaves out 'quoth he:' ii 2, 42, which rests merely on Malone's emendation: ii 4, 9 (But query, read 'answer't'): iii 4, 14 (Query, 'I doubt't not): iii 5, 126, where Q 1 omits 'I'll swear,' which is certainly like a player's insertion: iii 5, 137, where F 2 omits 'is:' in iii 1, 152, I would certainly omit 'cousin;' Lady Capulet is calling on the persons present, not on the dead, and 'O' is wanted before husband. Read then

O Prince, O husband, O the blood is spilt.

In iv 5, 1, F 2 omits 'she,' I would rather omit 'mistress.' In any case there can be at most nine Alexandrines in this play, not one of which occurs in the early Q 1, nor is one of them free from doubt. I infer that these early plays were carelessly revised (as indeed is evident from such passages as iii 5, 185) for the press, and that if Shakespeare admitted Alexandrines at all at this period, he did so very sparingly.

In *Merry Wives of Windsor* there are Alexandrines in iv 4, 8, 75, 70. The last should probably be read 'I'll go buy them vizards,' omitting 'and.' In Q 1 they occur in iv 4, 14, 15: iv 6, 28: v 5, 21. The last is clearly corrupt, and should be read 'If such a one you spy,' not 'can espy.'

In *Much Ado About Nothing* there are few Alexandrines,

and of these few some are dubious. In iv 1, 99, I would pronounce 'utter 'em' as two syllables: in iv 1, 115, omit the second 'uncle:' iv 1, 162, 172, are regular: so are v 1, 83, 87, 309.

In the *Two Gentleman of Verona* the instances are i 1, 80: iv 4, 113: ii 1, 114: iv 3, 4. In ii 2, 20, 'I come' should probably be omitted: in v 4, 71, pronounce

The private wound is deep'st: O time most 'curst.

In the *Merchant of Venice*, i 1, 50, 142: i 3, 138: ii 7, 5, 7, 9 (repeated in the casket inscriptions): ii 9, 25, 51: iii 2, 155: iv 1, 1, 320 (ten instances) are regular (in cesura). In i 3, 167,

Is not so estimable, profitable neither,

'estimable' occupies the time of two syllables (see S. Walker): ii 9, 28,

Which pries not to th' interior, but like the martlet.

'Which pries' may stand in a separate line, or the cesura may be after the eighth syllable. We have a Spenserian in iv 1, 4,

A stony adversary, | an inhuman wretch,

unless we read 'adverse.' In v 1, 25 (regular), query, should we omit 'a friend?'

In *King John* there are five instances at most (see my edition of the play).

In 1 *Henry IV*, ii 3, 65, v 2, 8, are regular. In i 1, 77, the Globe editors put 'In faith' in a separate line; but query, omit 'it is.' In iii 1, 138, I would transpose

> Come, you shall have Trent turn'd.
> I do not care:
> I'll give to any well-deserving friend
> Thrice so much land.

iii 1, 158, is corrupt in metre: iii 2, 2, is a Spenserian; but should 'at hand' be omitted? In iv 3, 12,

> As you, my lord, | or any Scot | that this day lives,

surely omit 'this day.' And yet compare *Romeo and Juliet*, ii 1, 15,

> He heareth not, | he stirreth not, | he moveth not,

where pronounce 'moo'th.' In v 4, 41, of course 'valiant' is a player's insertion to compliment the Shirley family.

In 2 *Henry IV.* Regular Alexandrines occur in iii 1, 5, 33, 96: iv 4, 15: iv 5, 159, 165; iii 1, 30, being the first line of a couplet, is doubtful. Some would pronounce

> Deny't to' a king. Then happy low, lie down,

but I cannot agree with them. In v 1, 20, certainly omit the second 'good morrow.'

In *Henry V* the regular instances are ii 2, 63, 168: iii 3, 5: iii 5, 24: iii 7, 168: iv Prol. 22, 28: iv 1, 322: iv 2, 23: iv 3, 18: iv 3, 33: iv 8, 86. In ii 2, 61, 'my lord' may be pronounced 'm' lord.' But I prefer to arrange

> Who are . . . . . [*With a long pause.*]
> The late commissioners? &c.

In *As You Like It*, true Alexandrines occur in i 3, 44: ii 1, 49, 52, 69: ii 7, 96: iii 5, 71, 74, 118.

In *Twelfth Night* we find them in i 1, 16: i 2, 1, 18: iii 3,

30: iv 3. 21: v 1, 75. In i 5. 312, 'Soft, soft!' should certainly be arranged in a separate line. In v 1, 219, arrange

> [*Pause.*] You throw
> A strange regard upon me; and by that, &c.

But part of the first line or more seems to me to have been lost here. In v 1, 359, read

> Which *here* were presupposed
> *Here* in the letter. Prithee, be content!

'Upon thee' has been mistakenly picked up from the next line by the compositor.

Up to this point, then (even if we suppose every doubtful instance to be genuine), we find that Shakespeare introduced only some half dozen or dozen Alexandrines in each play, and these usually (if not, as I believe, uniformly) of the regular form with the cesura in the middle, as the French write them. If there be any variation from this it is in the introduction of an occasional Spenserian line with cesura after the seventh syllable. But I doubt if these be not (in the early plays) all corruptions by the printer. To this statement there are no exceptions but the surreptitious olla-podrida of *Romeo and Juliet* and the *History of Richard II.* These exceptions I have explained as due to the fact that they were the first plays by Shakespeare that were published, and consequently are instances of careless correction for the press, and not of abnormal metrical treatment.

In *All's Well that Ends Well* the following are regular: i 1, 82: ii 5, 62, 76: iii 2, 53, 66: iii 5, 89: iii 7, 19: v 3, 13.

36, 209, 277, 305. In i 3, 225, either pause at 'Madam' or put 'tell true' in a separate line: ii 1, 36, and iii 4, 19, are Spenserian. In ii 1, 110, 122, 144, pronounce

And of | his old | expe | rience th' on | ly darling,
From her | inaid | able 'state | I say | we must not
When mir | acles have | by th' great | est been | denied.

This play marks the change to the third period: Alexandrines are more numerous: but the decisive characteristic is the increase of extra middle syllables. (See Table in Appendix.)

In *Measure for Measure* the regular instances are numerous and the change to the third period complete: i 1, 36: i 3, 37, 39: i 4, 5, 70: ii 2, 9, 12, 14, 41, 70: ii 4, 34, 105, 118, 123, 127, 141, 153: iii 1, 32, 51, 52, 53 [or are these a group of 7 lines of 3 feet each?], 61?, 81, 89, 116?, 150: iv 1, 52, 59, 68: iv 2, 77, 103: iv 3, 91, 137: iv 4, 29: iv 5, 6, 10: v 1, 8, 32, 42, 51, 56, 65, 67, 74, 101, 110, 112, 233, 256, 260, 379, 387, 392, 408, 463, 491, 498. With Spenserian cesura: in i 1, 56: ii 2, 183: iv 2, 86, pronounce and arrange

Matters of needful value: we shall write t' you.
To sin in loving virtue. ‖ Ne'er could the strumpet,
To qualify in others: were he mealed
With that which he corrects, then were he tyrannous.

IV 1, 65, is more doubtful, though we might pronounce "greed:" and in iv 2, 77, I would end the line at *Provost*, but any way the passage is harsh. In i 4, 43, pronounce certainly

To teeming foison: ‖ e'en so her plenteous womb.

In iv 3, 145, we have cesura at the eighth syllable unless we read *Marian's*, which is unlikely: and so in v 1, 299; but *poor souls* in this place should certainly stand in a line by itself.

In *Macbeth*, i 2, 37, 58, 64: i 3, 111: i 6, 10: ii 1, 3: ii 2, 30: ii 3, 88: iii 1, 45, 139: iii 2, 16: iii 3, 9, 11: iii 4, 2, 73, 121: iii 6, 29, 39, 49: iv 1, 88, 105, 153: iv 2, 30: iv 3, 8, 20, 97, 239: v 5, 17, are regular: iii 1, 91, 108: iv 2, 73, are not Alexandrines: they have the extra middle syllable, and should be printed 'We're men.' 'I'm one.' 'Whi'er should I fly?' II 2, 4, might be scanned

For a few | words. Ma'am | I will | Nought's had | All's spent.

III 6, 39, is faulty: a passage has probably been cut out here, if this very mysterious scene be Shakespeare's at all. In v 3, 5, pronounce 'consequence',' and in v 3, 37, 'm'lord,' or, if you please, call it a trisyllabic ending. There is no certain instance of a Spenserian Alexandrine in this play.

In *Hamlet*, i 1, 91, 53, 86, 142: i 2, 2, 90, 119, 140, 180: i 3, 24, 73, 85: i 4, 6, 13, 93, 142, 162, 177, 186: ii 1, 57, 112: iii 2, 58, 408: iii 3, 37: iii 4, 23, 88, 94, 131, 133: iv 3, 7: iv 4, 11: iv 5, 83, 102, 141, 179: iv 7, 9, 68, 77, 94, 181: v 2, 62, 68, are regular: iv 5, 84, is a Spenserian.

In hugger-mugger to inter him: poor Ophelia.

In *Othello*, i 1, 26, 27, 48, 138, 141, 158: i 2, 44, 71: i 3, 42, 54, 81, 89, 120, 189, 220, 248: ii 1, 17, 22, 65, 113, 197, 201, 203: ii 3, 53, 355: iii 1, 38, 49, 50: iii 3, 22, 58, 71, 76, 83, 132, 147, 161, 180, 183, 257, 270, 431: iii 4, 108, 196: iv 1, 46, 52, 75, 270: iv 2, 21, 62, 69: iv 3, 1, 18: v 1, 109, 123:

v 2, 13, 22, 39, 135, 139, 218, 234, 243, 312, 318, 348, are regular. In i 2, 10, read (omitting 'I' as so often in this phrase),

> I did full hard forbear him. But, 'pray you, sir.

In ii 3, 163, arrange

> You will be shamed for ever.
> What is the matter here? Zounds, I bleed still.
> I'm hurt to th' death. Hold for your lives! Hold ho!
> Lieutenant! Sir! Montano! Gentlemen!

In iii 3, 71, scan

> That came | a wooing | with yoú | and so man | y a time. |

In iii 3, 87, put 'farewell' in l. 86, or read 'Desdemon:' in iii 4, 40, omit 'and:' and in iii 4, 59, 'amiable' only occupies the time of two syllables. (See S. Walker.) In iv 2, 114, put 'I am' in the preceding line: iv 3, 34, is a true Spenserian, and the only certain one in the play.

In *King Lear*, i 1, 46, 94, 109, 134, 137, 150, 155, 198, 226, 228, 248, 250, 270: i 3, 23: i 4, 265, 322, 347, 351: ii 1, 119: ii 2, 79, 91, 121, 131, 144, 177: ii 4, 60, 121, 234: iii 2, 48, 67: iii 4, 176, 179: iii 6, 64: iii 7, 29: iv 1, 19: iv 2, 14, 28, 68: iv 3, 26: iv 4, 7: iv 5, 2: iv 6, 116, 147, 198: iv 7, 53, 54: v 1, 11: v 3, 25, 45, 208, 241, 295, 313, 444, are regular. In i 1, 139, 157: i 4, 223, there is to my ear a decided pause after the second syllable, but not strong enough to justify breaking the line into two. This is a new kind of Alexandrine which we shall find frequent in the plays of the fourth period. In i 2, 4, pronounce, I think, 'cúrious'ty' in three syllables: in ii 4, 157, 'unne'ss'ry' (so Walker): in iv 3, 44, there is a decided cesura after the fourth foot: this kind is not uncommon in the fourth period. IV 6, 256, is certainly Spenserian, so is v 3, 208. In v 3, 178, 271, it is doubtful if 'I know't' and 'Ha' should be put in lines by themselves. In this play, then, we find the turning point when the third period is ending.

In *Antony and Cleopatra*, i 1, 31: i 2, 84: i 4, 7, 47: i 5, 4, 34, 50: ii 1, 20, 31: ii 4, 9: ii 5, 31, 105: ii 7, 133: iii 1, 15, 27: iii 6, 15: iii 7, 76: iii 10, 29: iii 11, 73: iii 13, 82, 98: iv 3, 8: iv 4, 36: iv 9, 10, 33: iv 12, 48: iv 14, 18: v 2, 58, 150, are regular. In i 1, 59, pronounce 'I'm.' In i 2, 98, read 'on' for 'upon:' or put 'what worst' in a separate line. In i 4, 71, arrange

> So much as lank'd not. || 'Tis pity of him. | Let his shames
> Quickly drive him to Rome. 'Tis time we twain, &c.

The cesura is here at the ninth syllable. In ii 1, 38,

> The ne'er lust-wearied Antony. I cannot hope.

Possibly pronounce 'can't,' but I prefer making the line an Alexandrine. In ii 5, 113, it is doubtful whether 'her years' should begin or end a line: there is an Alexandrine in either case. In ii 6, 34, pronounce 'you've,' or rather 'y'have:' ii 7, 142, is doubtful as to arrangement. In iii 1, 35, we may pronounce 'whe'er,' but in l. 37 we have certainly a Spenserian Alexandrine. In iii 6, 20, arrange

> As 'tis reported, so. Let Rome be thus informed!
> Who queasy with his insolence already,
> Will their good thoughts call fróm him.

No writer of Shakespeare's time would have emphasized *will good*, and *him*, as modern editors do. In iii 6, 52, 76, the cesura is after the eighth syllable. In iii 13, 63, Antony is dissyllabic (as in i 1, 59: ii 1, 35 above). In iv 2, 40, cesura after ninth syllable. In iv 6, 11, arrange

> Upon himself. Alexas did revolt,
> And went to Jewry on affairs of Antony,
> There did persuade &c.

In iv 8, 20, 'yet ha' we' would be better in a separate line: iv 14, 80, is Spenserian: iv 14, 120, is quite un-Shakespearian, a fourteen-syllable line: v 2, 317, has cesura after fourth and eighth syllables. In this fourth period of Shakespeare's plays we find not only a much larger number of Alexandrines, but also lines with cesura at the second, fourth, fifth, seventh, ninth, or tenth syllables, shewing in this respect, as in others, a growing impatience of metrical rules: weak endings, female endings, broken lines, increase; and rhymes diminish; for the same reason.

In *Coriolanus* i 1, 196, 200: i 2, 37: i 4, 8: i 5, 21: i 7, 2: i 8, 7: ii 1, 220, 269: ii 3, 262: iii 1, 83, 112, 118, 144, 235: iii 2, 45: iv 1, 27: iv 2, 53: iv 5, 35: iv 6, 11, 46: v 1, 28: v 6, 64, 110, are regular: i 4, 5, 61: i 9, 58 [unless we read 'be't']: ii 3, 259: iii 1, 70: iv 5, 72: iv 7, 48: v 5, 6, are Spenserian: iii 1, 222 [unless we pronounce 'vi'lent']: v 1, 3, 45, 68: v 3, 148, have the cesura after the eighth syllable: i 10, 30, v 3, 35, after the tenth: iii 2, 138, after the second. In these two latter classes it is quite optional to arrange the odd foot at the beginning or end of the line separately. In iii 3, 49, we have a cesura after the eleventh syllable. This is so unprecedented that I would read

The warlike service he has done, consider!
Think on the wounds his body bears; which show, &c.

In i 7, 5, arrange

Fear not our care, sir! Hence, and shut the gates upon 's!

In ii 3, 232, arrange and pronounce

Th' appr'ension of his present portance, which
Most gibingly, ungravely, he did fashion, &c.

In *Cymbeline* i 1, 41 [but should not 'Posthumus' be omitted?], 46, 106: i 5, 44, 45: ii 2, 44: ii 4, 103: iii 1, 59: iii 2, 72; iii 3, 78: iii 4, 160; iv 2, 49, 81, 90, 100, 240: v 3, 70: v 4, 127: v 5, 120, 147, 239, are regular: i 1, 48: iii 4, 182: iv 2, 14, 107: iv 3, 42, are Spenserian: iii 1, 49: iv 2, 338: iv 3, 13, 15: v 2, 4: v 5, 347, have the cesura after the eighth syllable: iii 1, 68, after the ninth: i 1, 7: i 6, 48, 173: ii 4, 92: iv 3, 19, after the tenth. In ii 3, 60, pronounce

Th' one's Caius Lucius: a worthy fellow.

In ii 4, 96, arrange 'be pale' in l. 95. In ii 4, 125: iii 2, 33, pronounce 'hon'ble' 'med'c'n'ble' (see S. Walker). In iii 4, 3, arrange

Pisanio!
Man! Where's Posthumus, &c.

In the *Tempest* there are scarcely any Alexandrines: and very few extra syllables: but female and weak endings are numerous. This can only be accounted for on Mr. Staunton's hypothesis that the version we have is an abridgment: it is but two thirds of the length of the other fourth period plays. I 2, 102 [but, query, omit 'the' before 'duke?']: iii 1, 202, 236, 254:

ii 2, 74: iii 1, 31, 60: iii 2, 108: iii 3, 26, 102, are regular: i 2, 84, 236: ii 1, 36, are Spenserian. In i 2, 89, read 'dedicate',' not 'ded'cated,' as the reformer of English spelling and pronunciation who directs the New Shakspere Society would have it. In i 2, 105, arrange

> With all prerogative: hence his ambition
> Growing —— do'st hear? Your tale, sir, would cure deafness.

In ii 1, 283, pronounce 'three inch' of't:' in the next line 'doing' is one syllable. In i 2, 419, arrange

> A thing divine: for nothing natural, I
> E'er saw so noble. It goes on, I see.

In iv 1, 8, surely omit 'my:' the line as it stands is harsh in the extreme. In v 1, 8, the cesura is after the second syllable.

As *Winter's Tale* is undoubtedly the most developed and latest play of Shakespeare's in which there is no second hand visible, I have thought it desirable to print the Alexandrines *in extenso* with the cesuras marked. I have, in this instance, included all possibly doubtful cases in which the endings are probably trisyllabic, that the reader may have all the evidence before him. The preponderance (next to the regular lines) of lines with pause after the fifth foot is very striking. Where no cesura is marked, I believe the line to be one of trisyllabic feminine ending.

i 1, 21. Were there necessity in your request | although.
33. He's beat from his best ward. | Well said, Hermione.
45. Nay, but you will. I may not verily. Verily.
55. My pris'ner or my guest? | by your dread verily.
68. I'll no gainsaying. Press me not | beseech you so.

i 1, 108. The other for some while a friend. | Too hot, too hot.
117. As in a looking glass: | and then to sigh as 't were.
122. They say it is a copy out of mine. | Come, captain.
161. Will you take eggs for money? | No, my lord, | I'll fight.
227. Of head-piece extraordinary? | Lower messes
263. Are such allowed infirmities | that honesty
286. Of laughing with a sigh. | a note infallible
311. I'll give no blemish to her honour: none | My lord.
344. As friendship wears at feasts | keep with Bohemia.
352. What case stand I in? | I must be the poisoner.
371. That changeth thus his manners. | I dare not know, my lord.
391. As you are certainly a gentleman; | thereto.
408. That I think honourable: | therefore mark my counsel.
410. I mean to utter it | or both yourself and me.
454. Must it be violent? | and as he does conceive.
ii 1, 20. Into a goodly bulk: | good time encounter her.
53. So eas'ly open! | By his great authority.
107. With an aspect more favourable. | Good my lords.
152. As is a dead man's nose. | But I do see't and feel't.
164. Our forceful instigation! | Our prerogative.
182. Most piteous to be wild, | I have dispatcht in post.
185. Of stuft sufficiency. | Now from the oracle.
188. Shall stop or spur me. | Have I done well? | Well done, my lord?
ii 2, 11. Th' access of gentle visitors. | Is't lawful, pray you.
46. So meet for this great errand. | Please your ladyship.
53. ?
ii 3, 12. ?
21. And in his parties, his alliance. | Let him be.
42. Away with that audacious lady. | Antigonus.
102. His smiles.
137. And by good testimony, | or I'll seize thy life.
149. So to esteem of us: | and on our knees we beg.
167. To save the innocent: | anything possible.
189. Like offices of pity. | Sir, be prosperous.
iii 2, 5. Of being tyrannous, | since we so openly.

iii 2, 80. Sir.
87. Which to deny concerns more than avails. | For as.
209. Do not repent these things, | for they are heavier.
249. Shall be my recreation | so long as nature.
iii 3, 2. The deserts of Bohemia? Ay, my lord, | and fear.
iv 4, 375. Or Ethiopian's tooth, | or the fann'd snow that's bolted.
304. As you have ever been | my father's honour'd friend.
473. To die when I desire. | Why look you so upon me?
476. More straining on for plucking back; | not following.
518. I'll hear you by and by. | He's irremovable.
531. To have them recompensed | as thought on. Well, my lord.
541. Your discontenting father strive to qualify.
576. There is some sap in this. | A cause more promising.
592. She is i' th' rear our birth. | I cannot say 'tis pity.
672. He would not call me son. | Nay, you shall have no hat.
v i, 87. The fairest I have yet beheld, | desires access.
95. That e'er the sun shone bright on. | O Hermione.
111. The rarest of all women. | Go, Cleomenes.
v 3, 3. I did not well, I meant well. | All my services.
24. Thou art Hermione; | or, rather, thou art she.
47. The statue is but newly fixt. | T' colours | not dry.
128. Myself to see the issue. | There's time enough for that.
144. And take her by the hand; | whose worth and honesty.

In *Julius Cæsar*, i 1, 21: i 2, 114, 131: ii 1, 81, 100, 285: ii 2, 80, 118: ii 3, 10: ii 4, 32: iii 1, 116: iii 2, 1: iv 1, 10: iv 3, 129, 142, 157, 198, 273: v 1, 108: v 3, 7, 83, are all regular: and there is not an exceptional instance. This confirms my conclusion that a revision and abridgment of this play was made by a hand more formal and regular than Shakespeare's, probably after his death.

In the *Taming of the Shrew*, iv 1, 153,

Where's my spaniel Troilus? Sirrah, get you hence,

is a very doubtful instance. In iv 1, 155, pronounce 'acquaint'? iv 1, 215: iv 3, 43, 165: iv 5, 16: v 2, 18, 43, 175, are regular. All these are in Shakespeare's part. In the second author's, i 1, 210, 215: ii 1, 304, 343, 380, 405, 412: iii 2, 28: iv 2, 1: iv 4, 7, are regular: i 1, 72: i 2, 151: iv 2, 33: v 1, 121, are Spenserian.

In *Troylus and Cressida* (Troylus story), iii 1, 171: iii 2, 14: iv i, 9: iv 2, 6, 7, 14: iv 4, 5: v 2, 144, are regular: iii 2, 190: iv 3, 5, are Spenserian: iv 4, 71, &c., is a passage of doubtful arrangement. In iv 4, 118, 'Ilion' is dissyllabic. In the Ajax story, i 3, 3, 66, 80, 83, 168, 246, 357: ii 2, 46: ii 3, 134, 150, 188, 213: iii 3, 3, 30, 78, 107, 111, 123, 127, 149, 163, 169, 190, 194, 237: iv 5, 65, are regular: i 3, 331: iii 3, 153, are Spenserian. In the fragment at the end, v 5, 11: v 6, 30, are regular.

In *Timon of Athens* (Shakespeare's part), i 1, 62, 94, 139: ii 2, 12, 30, 154, 189, 241: iv 2, 8: iv 3, 2, 10, 81, 160, 241, 286, 370l, 417, 516: v 1, 108, 166, 205, 206, are regular: i 1, 10, is very harsh. Query, omit 'man!' In ii 2, 36, 'Pray you' should begin l. 37. In ii 2, 193, pronounce 'I'm wealthy:' iv 3, 48, is a Spenserian. In the part by the second hand, i 2, 161: iii 1, 64: iii 5, 29, 102, are regular: i 2, 219, 223, 229: iii 4, 58, have cesura at the eighth syllable: iii 3, 11: iii 4, 32, are Spenserian: iii 4, 68, 70, also should probably be arranged as verse: though they stand as prose in the Globe edition.

In *Pericles* (Shakespeare's part), iii 1, 6, 37: iii 3, 9, 17: iv i, 59: v 1, 31, 37, 53, 69, 72, 83, 175, are regular. In iii 4, 16, the cesura is after the fourth syllable: in iv 1, 50, after the eighth. But the arrangement of the lines in this corrupt play is dubious. I follow my own version, not the Globe, in this instance.

In the *Two Noble Kinsmen* there are no Alexandrines in Shakespeare's part: this can only be accounted for on the hypothesis that Fletcher expunged them: which requires not a joint contemporaneous authorship but a subsequent completion of the play by him. In Fletcher's own part the editors have left a few (from inadvertence?). In ii 1, 245, query, omit 'maintain'?: in ii 2, 16, arrange

> I know she's his: 'has a tongue will tame tempests.

In ii 2, 51, arrange

> Where he himself
> Will edify the duke most parlously
> In our behalf: he's excellent in the words, &c.

In iii 5, 93, end lines at 'way, have, sir.' In iv 1, 102, 'and fill' should be in a separate line. In v 1, 12, end lines at 'very, way, her, noise.' There is not a certain Alexandrine in the whole play.

In *Henry VIII* (Shakespeare's part), i 1, 27, 49: i 2, 124, 168, 179: ii 4, 88, 153: iii 2, 29, 137: v i, 107, 114, 141, are regular: i 2, 138, is Spenserian: i 1, 145, has cesura at the ninth syllable: i 2, 114; ii 3, 2; iii 2, 144, at the tenth. In i 2, 71,

> By learned approbation of the judges. If I am.

pronounce 'learn'd 'probation.' But the peculiar characteristic of this final play is the number of lines with cesura after the eighth syllable: ii 3, 16, 69: ii 4, 148, 163, 235: v 1, 668.

In Fletcher's part there are none certain. His admittance of trisyllabic feet to an extent unknown to Shakespeare deceives the ear, unless we come to this play fresh from reading plays entirely by Fletcher, such as *Bonduca*, for instance. Thus, in i 4, 104, pronounce

Good my lord card'nal, I've half a dozen healths.

In ii 1, 85,

'Gainst me that I can't take peace with: no black envy.

II 1, 56,

The king will venture at it. Ev'er the card'nal.

II 1, 131, and v 5, 64, are scarcely to be scanned on any hypothesis.

In 1 *Henry VI*, i 4, 17,

And e'en these three days have I watch'd, if I could see them.

Omit 'e'en these.' I 6, 11: iii 1, 13, 29, 96, 104, are regular. In iv 7, 52, end the lines at 'herald' and 'know.' In l. 94 pronounce

So we be rid o' em, do wi 'em what thou wilt.

There are no other instances in the play.

In 2 *Henry VI*, i 1, 208: i 4, 46: ii 1, 51, 135, 143 (prose in Globe edition): iii 1, 280, 326: iii 2, 119: iv 4, 7, are regular: iv 4, 37, a Spenserian. In iii 1, 8, pronounce 'per'mpt'ry:' iii 2, 278, 'we'll:' iv 10, 46, 'Saunder Iden.' I 1, 7, is irregular, as is often the case with proper name lists. IV 2, 145, has cesura after ninth syllable.

In 3 *Henry VI*, i 1, 55: i 4, 154: are probably accidental: ii 6, 82: iii 2, 110: iii 3, 163: iv 7, 77: v 2, 49, are regular.

In v 6, 81, put 'to wit' in a separate line. In iv 1, 84, perhaps read 'post' for 'messenger.'

It would be waste time to consider the *Contention* in detail unless one had the opportunity to edit and explain the causes of corruption in the present text. It must suffice to say that I so arrange it as to give forty-four Alexandrines in the *First Part*, and fifty-four in the *True Tragedy*.

In *Titus Andronicus*, i 1, 151: ii 3, 166: iii 1, 45, 185: iii 2, 66, 75: iv 1, 43, 122: iv 3, 121: iv 4, 103: v 2, 22, 152 (ending line at 'sons'): v 3, 40, are regular. In v 3. 91, 96, pronounce

And break my very utt'rance, e'en i' the time.
Then noble audit'ry, be 't known to you.

or,

Then, noble auditory, be it known t' ye.

In i 1, 201, put 'Titus' in a separate line, and in i 1, 203, read 'Saturnine.'

In *Edward III*, ii 2, 124, is the only Alexandrine in Shakespeare's part: iv 4, 45: v 1, 13, in the other part.

In *Richard III* the following instances occur in both versions, Q and F: v 3, 72, 187, 209 (but is this rightly arranged?), 281, 319 (but read ''ventures' as in Globe), 327. The lines containing ii 2, 127, are omitted in the Quarto. If we omit the consideration of the many (fifteen) lines in this play which are equally divided between two speakers, and which must be regarded rather as thirty lines of three feet each than as fifteen lines of six (look for instance at i 2, 192—203), not a single Alexandrine of the numerous instances in the Quarto is allowed to remain in the Folio. Two things are then clear: I. The end of the play, v 36—5, in which Q and F coincide, belongs to Q and not to F, the corrector having stopped his work at v 37. II. The corrector did not regard two speeches of three feet as making up one line; but wherever he found a line of six feet he ruthlessly expunged it.

But these corrections were made on a copy of the 1602 Quarto. Therefore Shakespeare, who at and after that date was enamoured of the Alexandrine and used it more frequently as his work went on, was not the corrector to whom we owe the Folio text, if that text be as usually supposed an *alteration* of the Quarto. On the other hand the number of Alexandrines in Q is so great that it is impossible that a play containing them should have come from the hand of Shakespeare *alone* in 1594—5, which is the latest date assignable to this play. The following are the instances in which the Folio cuts out Alexandrines from the Quarto: i 4, 59, 65, 97, 250, 277: ii 2, 24: ii 4, 25: iii 1, 37, 39, 71, 114, 158: iii 2, 46, 80, 110, 112, 114: iii 4, 9, 36: iv 1, 27: iv 2, 121: iv 3, 27: iv 4, 180, 275, 451, 512, 513, 523: v 3, 22. Of these nearly all are regular: iii 1, 114, has cesura after the seventh: iii 1, 158: iv 4, 275 (where one and half lines are omitted), after the eighth: iv 2, 42, is an Alexandrine in F, a line of four feet in Q: iv 2, 45, &c., is corrupt in both versions: probably the true reading is that of F if we omit 'know' and 'loving.' In iv 5, 7, F, there is a printer's error, arising from the repetition of 'withal' in l. 7 from l. 18, when lines 17, 18 were transposed (see the passage in both versions). In iii 1, 43, pronounce 'sanc'try.'

On the whole my explanation of the differences of the F

and Q versions is this. The original play of 1594–5 (by Shakespeare founded on Peele and Marlowe) stayed in MS. till 1602: Q (1598) being made up, like the Quartos of *Othello*, *Troylus and Cressida*, and 2 *Henry IV*, not from shorthand notes, but from a careless and hurried transcript of the prompter's copy surreptitiously obtained. The Folio version is printed from a copy of the 1602 Quarto, corrected from the original MS. by Shakespeare or under his supervision: but not in any way rewritten or enlarged or altered by him after its original production. In any case editors should mainly follow one version or the other when they have made up their minds as to which is the genuine one. Mongrel eclectic versions are the bane of criticism.

LOVE'S LABOUR'S LOST. [Original version, 1589-90: revised as in Q 1, 1597.]

Act	Scene	Total Lines	Prose	Blank	Heroic	Short Rhyme	Songs	Alternates	Sonnets	Doggerel	One Measure	Two Measure	Three Measure	Four Measure	Female Ending	Extra Syllable
I	1	317	143	41	67	2	—	64	—	—	—	—	—	—	2	—
	2	192	184	—	—	8	—	—			—	—		—	—	—
II	1	257	6	153	14	26	—		—	48	—	6	4		3	—
III	1	207	130	40	—	10			—	27	—	—	—		2	—
IV	1	151	49	13	29			4	—	52	—	3	1		—	
	2	173	139				—	6	14	14	—	—	—	—		
	3	386	24	108	107	20	—	72	28	25	—		2	—	4	
V	1	161	158	—		—	—	—	—	3				—	—	—
	2	941	189	262	333	—	36	96	—	18		3	4	—	15	—
		2785	1022	617	550	66	36	242	42	187	—	12	11	—	26	—

Note that the statements of date at the head of each table in brackets are not put forth as positive facts, but as the most probable hypotheses yet attained. I know from previous experience that I shall be accused of stating these hypotheses as facts in spite of this direct denial, nevertheless I think it right to make it.

The "extra syllable" in the last column is the "mid-line female-ending" before a pause, as in

Is prac | tice on | *ly.* || Give me | my ser | vant forth |

A MIDSUMMER NIGHT'S DREAM. [Written 1592: revised as in Q 1, 2, 1600.]

Act.	Scene.	Total Lines.	Prose.	Blank.	Heroic.	Short Rhyme.	Songs.	Alternates.	Sonnets.	Doggrel.	One Measure.	Two Measure.	Three Measure.	Four Measure.	Female Ending.	Extra Syllable.
I	1a	127	—	127	—	—	—	—	—	—	—	—	—	—	1	—
	1b	124	—	39	85	—	—	—	—	—	—	—	—	—	2	—
	2	114	106	—	—	8	—	—	—	—	—	—	—	—	—	—
II	1	268	—	180	76	12	—	—	—	—	—	—	—	—	8	—
	2	156	—	8	100	26	18	4	—	—	—	—	—	—	1	—
III	1	206	153	9	24	—	8	12	—	—	—	—	—	—	—	—
	2	463	—	151	228	46	—	16	—	—	—	22	—	—	18	—
IV	1a	107	40	31	16	16	—	4	—	—	—	—	—	—	3	—
	1b	110	21	78	9	—	—	—	—	—	—	2	—	—	6	—
	2	46	46	—	—	—	—	—	—	—	—	—	—	—	—	—
V	1a	377	127	106	36	48	—	60	—	—	—	—	—	—	20	1
	1b	68	—	—	—	68	—	—	—	—	—	—	—	—	—	—
		2166	493	729	574	224	26	96	—	—	—	24	—	—	59	1

COMEDY OF ERRORS. [Written 1592-3.]

Act	Scene	Total Lines	Prose.	Blank.	Heroic.	Short Rhyme.	Songs.	Alternates.	Sonnets	Doggrel.	One Measure.	Two Measure.	Three Measure	Four Measure.	Female Ending	Extra Syllable
I	1	159	—	146	10	—	—	—	—	—	1	2	—	—	3	—
	2	105	—	99	5	—	—	—	—	—	—	1	—	—	25	—
II	1	116	—	47	65	—	—	—	—	2	—	1	1	—	13	—
	2	221	68	105	45	—	—	—	—	2	—	—	1	—	12	—
III	1	123	—	43	8	—	—	—	—	72	—	—	—	—	9	—
	2	190	78	26	32	—	—	52	—	2	—	—	—	—	2	—
IV	1	113	—	109	4	—	—	—	—	—	—	—	—	—	22	—
	2	66	—	9	28	—	—	12	—	16	—	1	—	—	—	—
	3	97	45	46	5	—	—	—	—	—	—	1	—	—	10	—
	4	162	35	124	2	—	—	—	—	—	—	1	—	—	21	—
V	1	425	—	402	12	—	—	—	—	4	1	4	2	22	81	—
		1777	226	1156	216	—	—	64	—	98	2	11	4	22	178	—

RICHARD II. [c. 1593: revised 1597, with reference to Essex and Raleigh as Bolingbroke and Norfolk.]

Act.	Scene.	Total Lines.	Prose.	Blank.	Heroic.	Short Rhyme.	Songs.	Alternates.	Sonnets.	Doggrel.	One Measure.	Two Measure.	Three Measure.	Four Measure.	Female Ending.	Extra Syllable.
I	1	205	—	131	73	—	—	—	—	—	—	1	—	—	25	—
	2	74	—	57	16	—	—	—	—	—	—	—	—	1	7	—
	3	309	—	231	74	—	—	—	—	—	1	1	—	2	27	—
	4	65	—	60	—	—	—	—	—	—	2	1	—	2	7	—
II	1	300	—	244	50	—	—	4	—	—	—	—	2	—	26	—
	2	149	—	123	18	—	—	—	—	—	—	4	4	—	21	2
	3	171	—	158	4	—	—	—	—	—	—	—	7	2	34	6
	4	24	—	18	6	—	—	—	—	—	—	—	—	—	3	—
III	1	44	—	42	—	—	—	—	—	—	—	1	—	1	5	—
	2	218	—	179	38	—	—	—	—	—	—	—	1	—	10	—
	3	209	—	178	27	—	—	—	—	—	—	1	1	2	16	—
	4	107	—	81	18	—	—	—	—	—	—	4	3	1	7	1
IV	1	334	—	296	32	—	—	—	—	—	3	3	—	1	32	1
V	1	102	—	76	26	—	—	—	—	—	—	—	—	—	1	1
	2	117	—	101	8	—	—	—	—	—	1	5	2	—	17	4
	3	146	—	65	75	—	—	—	—	—	—	1	4	1	7	—
	4	11	—	8	2	—	—	—	—	—	1	—	—	—	—	—
	5	119	—	97	17	—	—	—	—	—	—	2	1	2	6	2
	6	52	—	9	41	—	—	—	—	—	—	—	1	1	7	—
		2756	—	2174	525	—	—	4	—	—	8	23	26	16	258	18

ROMEO AND JULIET, Q 1. [Written 1591: partly revised 1596: completely revised before 1599, as in Q 2: Q 1 is a mixture of the 1591 original play and the revision of 1596.]

Act.	Scene.	Total Lines.	Prose.	Blank.	Heroic.	Short Rhyme.	Songs.	Alternates.	Sonnets.	Doggrel.	One Measure.	Two Measure.	Three Measure.	Four Measure.	Female Ending.	Extra Syllable.
I	1	135	42	51	40	—	—	—	—	—	—	—	2	—	2	—
	2	95	16	32	36	—	—	8	—	—		—	3		9	—
	3	67	3	60	4	—	—	—	—	—		—	—	—	7	—
	4	93	—	74	16	—	—	—	—			1	1	1	2	—
	5	113	—	62	30	—	—	16	—		1	1	4	1	3	
II	1, 2	203	—	173	20	—	—	—	—		2	3	3	2	5	4
	3	87	—	78	8	—	—		—		—	1	—		6	1
	4	101	144	15		—				—	—	—	1	1	—	—
	5	42	14	20	2	—	—		—	—	—	—	—		—	1
	6	28	14	12		—		—	—	—	1	1			—	—
III	1	147	—	110	32	—	—	—	—	—	—	1	4	—		—
	2	59	—	50	2	—	—	4	—			1	2		4	3
	3	138	—	130	4	—	—	—	—	—		2	1	1	8	3
	4	20	—	22	—	—	—	—			1	—	1	2	6	
	5	190		160	16	—		—	—		—	4	3	7	9	6
IV	1	91		80	10	—		—			—			1	9	1
	2	40	8	30	—	—		—				2			4	
	3	28	2	24	2	—				—					4	—
	4	20		17		—		—	—			1	2		—	—
	5	88	16	58	10	—			—	—	1	2	1		1	1
V	1	64		58	2	—		—		—	—	—	3	1	3	1
	2	20		10	—	—		—		—	—	2	1	1	1	
	3	219	—	192	14	—		—		—	1	4	5	3	20	3
		2156	259	1530	248	—	—	28	—		7	26	37	21	103	24

ROMEO AND JULIET, Q 2.

Act.	Scene.	Total Lines.	Prose.	Blank.	Heroic.	Short Rhyme.	Songs.	Alternates.	Sonnets.	Doggrel.	One Measure.	Two Measure.	Three Measure.	Four Measure.	Female Ending.	Extra Syllable.
Prologue		14	—	—	—	—	—	—	14	—	—	—	—	—	—	—
I	1	244	65	115	55	—	—	4	—	—	1	2	2	—	2	—
	2	106	17	40	38	—	—	8	—	—	1	—	2	—	4	—
	3	106	—	85	18	—	—	—	—	—	—	3	—	—	7	—
	4	114	—	99	14	—	—	—	—	—	1	—	—	—	1	—
	5	146	43	48	36	—	—	16	—	—	1	1	1	—	2	1
Chorus		14	—	—	—	—	—	—	14	—	—	—	—	—	—	—
II	1	42	—	36	6	—	—	—	—	—	—	—	—	—	2	1
	2	190	—	168	20	—	—	—	—	—	—	—	2	—	7	—
	3	94	—	—	94	—	—	—	—	—	—	—	—	—	—	—
	4	233	208	19	2	—	—	—	—	—	—	1	3	—	1	—
	5	80	9	62	6	—	—	—	—	—	1	1	1	—	—	—
	6	37	—	33	4	—	—	—	—	—	—	—	—	—	3	—
III	1	202	63	89	44	—	—	—	—	—	—	2	4	—	9	1
	2	143	—	123	12	—	—	8	—	—	—	—	—	—	9	—
	3	175	—	162	10	—	—	—	—	—	2	—	1	—	8	1
	4	36	—	35	—	—	—	—	—	—	1	—	—	—	8	—
	5	242	—	217	20	—	—	—	—	—	3	1	—	1	26	4
IV	1	126	—	119	6	—	—	—	—	—	—	—	1	—	11	—
	2	47	—	46	—	—	—	—	—	—	—	—	1	—	9	1
	3	58	—	56	—	—	—	—	—	—	1	—	1	—	8	—
	4	27	—	23	—	—	—	—	—	—	1	2	—	1	5	—
	5	149	50	83	10	—	4	—	—	—	—	1	—	1	6	1
V	1	86	—	84	2	—	—	—	—	—	—	—	—	—	6	1
	2	30	—	28	2	—	—	—	—	—	—	—	—	—	1	—
	3	310	—	282	18	—	—	10	—	—	—	—	—	—	33	1
		3051	455	2052	417	—	4	46	28	—	13	14	19	3	168	12

TWO GENTLEMEN OF VERONA. [Written 1593-4.]

Act.	Scene.	Total Lines.	Prose.	Blank.	Heroic.	Short Rhyme.	Songs.	Alternates.	Sonnets.	Doggrel.	One Measure.	Two Measure.	Three Measure.	Four Measure.	Female Ending.	Extra Syllable.
I	1	161	72	79	6	—	—	—	—	4	—	—	—	—	7	—
	2	140	—	101	20	—	—	—	—	2	3	1	13	—	13	1
	3	91	—	80	—	—	—	8	—	—	—	1	2	—	13	—
II	1	182	126	39	2	—	—	—	—	12	1	2	—	—	8	2
	2	21	16	—	4	—	—	—	—	—	—	—	1	—	2	—
	3	65	65	—	—	—	—	—	—	—	—	—	—	—	—	—
	4	214	48	160	2	—	—	—	—	—	—	1	3	—	41	—
	5	63	63	—	—	—	—	—	—	—	—	—	—	—	—	—
	6	43	—	41	2	—	—	—	—	—	—	—	—	—	9	—
	7	90	—	89	—	—	—	—	—	—	—	1	—	—	15	—
III	1	395	144	218	18	—	—	11	—	—	—	1	1	2	47	—
	2	98	—	95	—	—	—	—	—	—	—	2	1	—	19	—
IV	1	76	—	72	—	—	—	—	—	—	1	2	1	—	10	—
	2	141	58	66	—	—	15	—	—	—	—	1	1	—	20	—
	3	46	—	46	—	—	—	—	—	—	—	—	—	—	5	—
	4	210	67	134	—	—	—	—	—	—	3	2	3	1	33	1
V	1	12	—	12	—	—	—	—	—	—	—	—	—	—	2	—
	2	56	—	42	—	—	—	—	—	—	—	—	11	3	7	—
	3	15	—	11	2	—	—	—	—	—	1	1	—	—	—	1
	4	173	—	146	20	—	—	—	—	—	—	2	4	1	18	—
		2292	659	1431	76	—	15	19	—	18	9	17	41	7	269	5

THE MERCHANT OF VENICE. [Written 1595 and revised 1598.]

Act.	Scene.	Total Lines.	Prose.	Blank.	Heroic.	Short Rhyme.	Songs.	Alternates.	Sonnets.	Doggrel.	One Measure.	Two Measure.	Three Measure.	Four Measure.	Female Ending.	Extra Syllable.
I	1	185	7	168	4	—	—	—	—	2	—	2	1	1	18	5
	2	145	145	—	—	—	—	—	—	—	—	—	—	—	—	—
	3	183	40	133	6	—	—	—	—	—	1	1	2	—	19	1
II	1	46	—	42	4	—	—	—	—	—	—	—	—	—	5	1
	2	215	165	47	—	—	—	—	—	—	1	—	2	—	12	—
	3	21	5	12	2	—	—	—	—	—	—	1	1	—	4	—
	4	40	—	37	—	—	—	—	—	—	—	3	—	—	5	—
	5	57	12	33	6	2	—	—	—	—	—	3	1	—	6	—
	6	68	—	62	4	—	—	—	—	—	—	1	1	—	2	—
	7	79	—	61	6	10	—	—	—	—	—	1	1	—	15	1
	8	53	—	53	—	—	—	—	—	—	—	—	—	—	16	—
	9	101	—	76	7	16	—	—	—	—	1	—	1	—	9	2
III	1	136	136	—	—	—	—	—	—	—	—	—	—	—	—	—
	2	329	8	267	26	6	9	4	—	—	2	2	3	2	45	11
	3	36	—	35	—	—	—	—	—	—	—	—	1	—	6	—
	4	84	—	80	2	—	—	—	—	—	—	1	1	—	16	3
	5	95	69	26	—	—	—	—	—	—	—	—	—	—	6	1
IV	1	457	17	433	2	—	—	—	—	—	1	1	3	—	82	—
	2	19	—	16	2	—	—	—	—	—			1	—	4	1
V	1	307	—	291	14	—	—	—	—	—	1	—	1	—	55	6
		2656	604	1872	85	34	9	4	—	2	7	16	20	3	325	32

HENRY IV, Part I. [Written 1597: revised, with Falstaff for Oldcastle, before February, 1598.]

Act.	Scene.	Total Lines.	Prose.	Blank.	Heroic.	Short Rhyme.	Songs.	Alternates.	Sonnets.	Doggrel.	One Measure.	Two Measure.	Three Measure.	Four Measure.	Female Ending.	Extra Syllable.
I	1	108	—	105	—	—	—	—	—	—	—	2	—	1	5	2
	2	241	218	21	2	—	—	—	—	—	—	—	—	—	—	—
	3	302	—	279	14	—	—	—	—	—	5	—	3	1	13	4
II	1	106	106	—	—	—	—	—	—	—	—	—	—	—	—	—
	2	118	107	8	2	—	—	—	—	—	—	1	—	—	1	—
	3	120	39	70	6	—	—	—	—	—	1	—	2	2	4	1
	4	602	579	21	—	—	—	—	—	—	1	—	—	1	1	—
III	1	271	20	228	10	—	—	—	—	—	3	3	4	3	23	3
	2	180	—	175	4	—	—	—	—	—	—	—	—	1	7	1
	3	230	224	2	4	—	—	—	—	—	—	—	—	—	—	—
IV	1	136	—	120	12	—	—	—	—	—	—	1	2	1	9	2
	2	86	84	—	—	—	—	—	—	2	—	—	—	—	—	—
	3	113	—	108	2	—	—	—	—	—	1	1	—	1	3	—
	4	41	—	33	2	—	—	4	—	—	—	1	1	—	5	1
V	1	143	25	114	2	—	—	—	—	—	—	1	—	1	5	1
	2	101	—	97	—	—	—	—	—	—	1	1	—	2	3	1
	3	65	18	38	4	—	—	—	—	—	2	2	1	—	5	—
	4	169	44	108	8	—	—	—	—	—	2	3	2	2	7	3
	5	44	—	34	8	—	—	—	—	—	—	1	1	—	1	—
		3176	1464	1561	80	—	—	4	—	2	16	17	16	16	92	19

HENRY IV, Part 2. [Written 1598.]

Act.	Scene.	Total Lines.	Prose.	Blank.	Heroic.	Short Rhyme.	Songs.	Alternates.	Sonnets.	Doggrel.	One Measure.	Two Measure.	Three Measure.	Four Measure.	Female Ending.	Extra Syllable.
Induction		40	—	36	4	—	—	—	—	—	—	—	—	—	1	—
I	1	215	—	211	4	—	—	—	—	—	—	—	—	—	14	2
	2	278	278	—	—	—	—	—	—			—	—	—	—	—
	3	110	—	106	4	—	—	—	—	—	—	—	—	—	13	2
II	1	209	196	6	—	—	—	—	—	—	—	—	7	—	—	—
	2	196	196	—	—	—	—	—	—	—	—	—	—	—	—	—
	3	68	—	66	2	—	—	—	—	—	—	—	—	—	10	1
	4	421	381	12	—	—	—	28	Pistol	—	—	—	—	—	3	—
III	1	108	—	98	8	—	—	—	—	—	—	1	1	—	15	1
	2	358	358	—	—	—	—	—	—	—	—	—	—	—	—	—
IV	1	228	—	227	—	—	—	—	—	—	—	—	1	—	32	2
	2	123	—	111	10	—	—	—	—	—	—	1	1	—	30	2
	3	142	121	18	2	—	—	—	—	—	—	—	1	—	2	—
	4	132	—	130	—	—	—	—	—	—	—	—	2	—	27	3
	5	241	—	222	12	—	—	—	—	—	—	5	2	—	32	5
V	1	98	98	—	—	—	—	—	—	—	—	—	—	—	—	—
	2	145	—	140	2	—	—	—	—	—	1	2	—	—	35	2
	3	147	108	—	—	—	15	24	Pistol	—	—	—	—	—	—	—
	4	35	35	—	—	—	—	—	—	—	—	—	—	—	—	—
	5	115	49	42	6	—	—	12	Pistol	—	2	4	—	—	7	1
Epilogue.		37	37	—	—	—	—	—	—	—	—	—	—	—	—	—
		3446	1857	1425	54	—	15	64	Pistol	—	3	13	15	—	221	21

HENRY V. [Written 1599. Q 1 is a surreptitious version.]

Act.	Scene.	Total Lines.	Prose.	Blank.	Heroic.	Short Rhyme.	Songs.	Alternates.	Sonnets.	Doggrel.	One Measure.	Two Measure.	Three Measure.	Four Measure.	Female Ending.	Extra Syllable.
Prologue		34	—	30	4	—	—	—	—	—	—	—	—	—	2	1
I	1	98	—	94	2	—	—		—	—	1	1	—	—	20	1
	2	340	—	296	8	2	—		—	—		—	3	1	54	4
Prologue		42	—	37	4	—	—	—	—				—	1	4	—
II	1	134	88	—	—	—	—	46 Pst	—			—	—	—	—	—
	2	195	6	182	2	—	—	—	—	—	1	—	1	1	48	8
	3	67	51	—	—			16 Pst	—			—	—	—	—	—
	4	146	—	145	—	—	—	—	—	—	—	1	—	—	42	—
Prologue		35	—	33	2	—	—	—	—	—	—	—	—	—	13	—
III	1	34		32	2	—		—	—	—	—	—	—	—	7	—
	2	153	139	—	—	—	S	6 Pst	—	—	—	—	—	—	—	—
	3	58	—	54	4	—		—	—	—	—	—	—	—	12	—
	4	144	144	—	—	—		—	—	—	—	—	—	—	—	—
	5	68	—	64	2	—		—	—	—	—	1	1	—	12	—
	6	181	123	35	—	—	—	21 Pst	—	—	1	1	—		9	—
	7	169	167	—	2	—	—	—	—	—	—	—	—	—	—	—
Prologue		53	—	51	2	—	—	—	—	—	—	—		—	2	—
IV	1	325	195	105	4	—	—	17 Pst	—	—	1	2	1	—	16	3
	2	63	—	58	4	—	—	—	—	—		1	—	—	3	—
	3	132	—	125	4	—	—	—	—	—	—	1	2	—	28	2
	4	82	52	—	—	—	—	30 Pst	—	—	—	—	—	—		—
	5	23	—	20	2	—	—	—	—	—	—	—	—	1	4	—
	6	38	—	37	—	—		—	—	—	—	1	—	—	4	—
	7	191	133	55	—	—		—	—	—	—	2	1	—	11	—
	8	131	79	48	2	—		—	—	—	—	1	1	—	11	3
Prologue		45	—	43	2	—	—	—	—	—		—	—	—	6	—
V	1	94	71	—	2	—	—	21 Pst	—	—		—	—	—	—	—
	2	502	119	374	8	—	—	—	—	—		—	1	—	28	3
Epilogue		14	—	—	—	—	—	—	14	—		—	—	—	—	
		3559	1367	1918	62	2	8	157 P	14	—	4	12	11	4	336	25

Q 1 is so corrupt that it is not worth tabulating. The total results are given in my Shakespeare manual.

MERRY WIVES OF WINDSOR, Q 1. [Written 1592: rewritten 1599: revised as in F, c. 1604. Q 1 is a mixture of the 1592 and 1599 versions.]

Act.	Scene.	Total Lines.	Prose.	Blank.	Heroic.	Short Rhyme.	Songs.	Alternates.	Sonnets.	Doggrel.	One Measure.	Two Measure.	Three Measure.	Four Measure.	Female Ending.	Extra Syllable.
III	4	—	—	15	2			—	—	—	—	—			2	
IV	4	—	—	52	12	—	—	—	—	—	—	—		2	5	—
	6	—	—	34	—	—	—	—	—	—	—	1	—		10	—
V	4	—	—	47	20	—	—	—	—	—	—	—	—	—	2	—
		(fair ies)		—	—	34	—	8	—	—	—	—	—	—	—	—
		—	—	148	34	34	—	8	—	—	—	1	—	2	19	—

The rest of the play is prose. Total number of lines 7395.

MERRY WIVES OF WINDSOR, F.

Act.	Scene.	Total Lines.	Prose.	Blank.	Heroic.	Short Rhyme.	Songs.	Alternates.	Sonnets.	Doggrel.	One Measure.	Two Measure.	Three Measure.	Four Measure.	Female Ending.	Extra Syllable.
I	1	—	—	—	—	—	—	6	Pistol	—	—	—	—	—	—	—
	3	—	—	5	2	4	—	26	,,	—	—	—	—	—	1	—
II	1	—	—	—	—	5	—	12	,,	—	—	—	—	—	—	—
	2	—	—	—	—	—	—	7	,,	—	—	—	—	—	—	—
III	1	—	—	—	—	—	4	—	—	—	—	—	—	—	—	—
	4	—	—	53	—	—	—	—	—	—	—	—	3	—	13	—
IV	4	—	—	71	2	—	—	—	—	—	1	2	—	—	15	3
	6	—	—	53	—	—	—	—	—	—	—	—	—	—	17	4
V	3	—	—	—	2	—	—	—	—	—	—	—	—	—	—	—
	5	—	—	25	6	—	—	—	—	—	—	1	—	—	8	1
		(fair	ies)	—	53	—	10	—	—	—	—	—	—	—	—	—
		—	—	207	65	9	14	51	Pistol	—	1	3	3	—	54	8

The rest of the play is prose. Total number of lines 3029.

MUCH ADO ABOUT NOTHING. [Written as Love's Labour's Won 1590 : rewritten 1599 as we have it.]

Act	Scene	Total Lines.	Prose.	Blank.	Heroic.	Short Rhyme.	Songs.	Alternates.	Sonnets.	Doggrel.	One Measure.	Two Measure.	Three Measure.	Four Measure.	Female Ending.	Extra Syllable.
I	1	—	—	39	—	—	—	—	—	—	—	—	—	—	5	—
II	1	—	—	11	—	—	—	—	—	—	—	—	—	—	2	—
	3	—	—	19	—	—	12	—	—	—	—	—	2	—	4	—
III	1	116	—	103	4	—	—	8	—	—	—	—	1	—	33	3
IV	1	—	—	215	2	—	—	4	—	—	—	3	7	—	47	4
V	1	—	—	147	4	—	—	—	—	—	1	2	3	2	28	2
	2	—	—	—	—	—	4	—	—	—	—	—	—	—	—	—
	3	33	—	2	—	—	20	10	—	—	—	1	—	—	1	—
	4	—	—	82	8	—	—	—	—	—	—	1	2	1	25	2
		—	—	618	18	—	36	22	—	-	1	7	15	3	145	11

The rest of the play is prose. Total number of lines 2823.

AS YOU LIKE IT. [Written 1598.]

Act.	Scene.	Total Lines.	Prose.	Blank.	Heroic.	Short Rhyme.	Songs.	Alternates.	Sonnets.	Doggrel.	One Measure.	Two Measure.	Three Measure.	Four Measure.	Female Ending.	Extra Syllable.
I	1	180	180	—	—	—	—	—	—	—	—	—	—	—	—	—
	2	301	236	58	4	—	—	—	—	—	—	—	3	—	19	1
	3	140	41	93	2	—	—	—	—	—	—	—	3	1	24	3
II	1	69	—	69	—	—	—	—	—	—	—	—	—	—	8	1
	2	21	—	21	—	—	—	—	—	—	—	—	—	—	9	—
	3	76	—	62	12	—	—	—	—	—	1	—	1	—	17	1
	4	100	37	50	6	2	—	—	—	—	—	2	3	—	13	2
	5	65	41	—	—	—	24	—	—	—	—	—	—	—	—	—
	6	19	19	—	—	—	—	—	—	—	—	—	—	—	—	—
	7	183	—	157	6	—	16	—	—	—	—	2	2	—	35	6
III	1	18	—	17	—	—	—	—	—	—	—	—	1	—	6	—
	2	456	396	—	—	50	—	10	—	—	—	—	—	—	—	—
	3	109	101	—	—	—	6	—	—	2	—	—	—	—	—	—
	4	62	49	9	4	—	—	—	—	—	—	—	—	—	1	1
	5	139	4	122	8	—	—	—	—	—	—	2	2	1	29	3
IV	1	224	224	—	—	—	—	—	—	—	—	—	—	—	—	—
	2	19	10	—	—	—	9	—	—	—	—	—	—	—	—	—
	3	184	42	119	—	20	—	—	—	—	—	3	—	—	26	2
V	1	69	69	—	—	—	—	—	—	—	—	—	—	—	—	—
	2	134	102	20	—	—	—	—	—	—	—	—	12	—	11	1
	3	43	25	—	—	—	18	—	—	—	—	—	—	—	—	—
	4	204	79	74	16	2	30	—	—	—	—	2	1	—	32	1
Epilogue		24	24	—	—	—	—	—	—	—	—	—	—	—	—	—
		2839	1679	871	58	74	103	10	—	2	1	11	28	2	230	22

TWELFTH NIGHT. [Viola story first written 1594 : complete play as we have it 1600.]

Act.	Scene.	Total Lines.	Prose.	Blank.	Heroic.	Short Rhyme.	Songs.	Alternates.	Sonnets.	Doggrel.	One Measure.	Two Measure.	Three Measure.	Four Measure.	Female Ending.	Extra Syllable.
I	1	41	—	36	4	—	—	—	—	—	1	—	—	—	5	3
	2	64	—	51	6	—	—	—	—	—	2	2	3	—	14	1
	3	151	151	—	—	—	—	—	—	—	—	—	—	—	—	—
	4	42	9	31	2	—	—	—	—	—	—	—	—	—	6	—
	5	330	262	57	6	—	—	—	—	—	1	1	3	—	9	4
II	1	49	44	3	2	—	—	—	—	—	—	—	—	—	1	—
	2	42	17	21	4	—	—	—	—	—	—	—	—	—	4	—
	3	208	196	—	—	—	12	—	—	—	—	—	—	—	—	—
	4	127	16	74	10	—	16	—	—	—	—	5	5	1	14	4
	5	227	219	—	—	8	—	—	—	—	—	—	—	—	—	—
III	1	176	96	55	18	—	—	—	—	—	—	2	4	1	10	1
	2	90	90	—	—	—	—	—	—	—	—	—	—	—	—	—
	3	48	—	46	—	—	—	—	—	—	—	1	1	—	17	1
	4	433	343	63	18	—	—	—	—	—	1	3	4	1	20	4
IV	1	69	31	25	8	—	—	—	—	—	—	4	1	—	1	—
	2	141	129	—	—	—	12	—	—	—	—	—	—	—	—	—
	3	35	—	30	4	—	—	—	—	—	—	—	—	1	8	1
V	1	417	128	232	26	—	20	—	—	—	—	4	6	1	58	9
		2690	1731	724	108	8	60	—	—	—	5	22	27	5	167	28

ALL'S WELL THAT ENDS WELL. [Written early : rewritten c. 1601-2.]

Act.	Scene.	Total Lines.	Prose.	Blank.	Heroic.	Short Rhyme.	Songs.	Alternates.	Sonnets.	Doggrel.	One Measure.	Two Measure.	Three Measure.	Four Measure.	Female Ending.	Extra Syllable.
I	1	244	148	75	16	—	—	—	—	—	2	2	—	1	17	1
	2	76	—	75	—	—	—	—	—	—	—	—	1	—	20	5
	3	262	133	92	16	—	12	4	—	—	1	1	3	—	41	4
II	1	213	18	107	82	—	—	—	—	—	—	1	5	—	34	8
	2	74	65	7	—	—	—	—	—	—	—	2	—	—	1	2
	3	317	146	109	52	—	—	—	—	—	1	2	5	2	28	3
	4	57	33	24	—	—	—	—	—	—	—	—	—	—	3	1
	5	97	44	47	4	—	—	—	—	—	1	—	1	—	9	1
III	1	23	—	19	2	—	—	—	—	—	—	1	1	—	7	1
	2	132	39	84	2	—	—	—	—	—	—	3	4	—	17	2
	3	11	—	9	2	—	—	—	—	—	—	—	—	—	1	1
	4	42	—	26	2	—	—	—	14	—	—	—	—	—	5	3
	5	104	35	61	—	—	—	—	—	—	—	3	4	1	22	7
	6	125	114	11	—	—	—	—	—	—	—	—	—	—	4	2
	7	48	—	42	4	—	—	—	—	—	—	1	1	—	16	2
IV	1	104	88	13	—	—	—	—	—	—	—	—	2	1	6	1
	2	76	—	62	12	—	—	—	—	—	—	—	2	—	12	7
	3	376	357	5	9	—	—	4	—	—	—	1	—	—	1	—
	4	36	—	32	4	—	—	—	—	—	—	—	—	—	15	1
	5	112	112	—	—	—	—	—	—	—	—	—	—	—	—	—
V	1	38	—	28	4	—	—	—	—	—	1	2	3	—	6	2
	2	59	59	—	—	—	—	—	—	—	—	—	—	—	—	—
	3	334	46	248	34	—	—	—	—	—	—	2	4	—	84	12
Epilogue		6	—	—	6	—	—	—	—	—	—	—	—	—	—	—
		2966	1437	1176	251	—	12	8	14	—	6	21	36	5	349	66

MEASURE FOR MEASURE. [1603.]

Act.	Scene.	Total Lines.	Prose.	Blank.	Heroic.	Short Rhyme.	Songs.	Alternates.	Sonnets.	Doggrel.	One Measure.	Two Measure.	Three Measure.	Four Measure.	Female Ending.	Extra Syllable.
I	1	84	—	77	2	—	—	—	—	—	—	1	4	—	28	4
	2	198	133	59	—	[?3]	—	—	—	—	—	—	6	—	10	2
	3	54	—	51	2	—	—	—	—	—	—	1	—	—	16	5
	4	90	—	85	—	—	—	—	—	—	—	2	3	—	20	5
II	1	290	236	42	8	—	—	—	—	—	1	—	3	—	15	3
	2	187	—	169	2	—	—	—	—	—	1	6	6	3	38	12
	3	41	—	35	—	—	—	—	—	—	—	1	4	1	14	3
	4	187	—	163	6	—	—	—	—	—	3	4	8	3	39	11
III	1	281	130	137	2	—	—	—	—	—	—	3	7	2	25	10
	2	296	246	18	6	22	—	—	—	—	—	—	3	1	2	1
IV	1	76	10	51	6	—	6	—	—	—	—	1	2	—	8	3
	2	226	166	45	12	—	—	—	—	—	—	1	2	—	6	1
	3	190	101	74	5	—	—	—	—	—	1	3	6	—	16	5
	4	37	22	13	2	—	—	—	—	—	—	—	—	—	1	3
	5	13	—	13	—	—	—	—	—	—	—	—	—	—	3	—
	6	15	—	14	—	—	—	—	—	—	—	—	1	—	5	2
V	1	545	90	424	8	—	—	—	—	—	—	6	13	4	131	28
		2810	1134	1470	61	22	6	—	—	—	6	29	68	14	377	98

MACBETH. [Written before 1596: rewritten 1603-4: abridged and interpolated as we have it after 1613.]

Act.	Scene.	Total Lines.	Prose.	Blank.	Heroic.	Short Rhyme.	Songs.	Alternates.	Sonnets.	Doggrel.	One Measure.	Two Measure.	Three Measure.	Four Measure.	Female Ending.	Extra Syllable.
I	1	[10	—	[1	—	[9]	—	—	—	—	—	—	—	—	—	—
	2	67	—	59	4	—	—	—	—	—	—	4	—	—	10	1
	3a	[37]	—	[13?]	—	[24]	—	—	—	—	—	—	—	—	—	—
	3b	119	—	101	2	—	[11	lines	Witches]		—	—	4	1	32	6
	4	58	—	46	8	—	—	—	—	—	—	—	2	2	17	5
	5	74	15	53	4	—	—	—	—	—	—	—	2	—	17	5
	6	31	—	29	—	—	—	—	—	—	—	1	—	1	14	1
	7	82	—	79	2	—	—	—	—	—	—	—	—	1	18	3
II	1	64	—	55	4	—	—	—	—	—	—	2	2	1	15	—
	2	74	—	70	—	—	—	—	—	—	1	—	3	—	25	6
	3	152	45	92	4	—	—	—	—	—	—	4	6	1	27	4
	4	41	—	35	4	—	—	—	—	—	—	2	—	—	7	2
III	1	142	—	134	2	—	—	—	—	—	1	3	1	1	34	6
	2	56	—	43	8	—	—	—	—	—	—	—	5	—	8	3
	3	22	—	19	—	—	—	—	—	—	1	—	2	—	4	—
	4	144	—	128	8	—	—	—	—	—	—	3	5	—	29	9
	5	[36]	—	[2]	—	[34]	—	—	—	—	—	—	—	—	—	—
	6	49	—	49	—	—	—	—	—	—	—	—	—	—	11	3
IV	1	131	—	73	12	37	—	—	—	—	—	2	4	3	8	—
		[25]			[8]	[17]										
	2	85	20	60	—	—	—	—	—	—	—	2	3	—	18	3
	3	240	—	229	4	—	—	—	—	—	—	1	4	2	66	9
V	1	87	78	7	2	—	—	—	—	—	—	—	—	—	4	2
	2	31	—	28	2	—	—	—	—	—	—	—	1	—	9	2
	3	62	—	51	6	—	—	—	—	—	1	1	3	—	13	3
	4	21	—	16	4	—	—	—	—	—	—	—	1	—	8	1
	5	52	—	44	6	—	—	—	—	—	—	2	—	—	7	—
	6	10	—	6	4	—	—	—	—	—	—	—	—	—	1	1
	7	29	—	24	2	—	—	—	—	—	—	—	3	—	6	—
	8	75	—	65	8	—	—	—	—	—	—	2	—	—	12	3
		1998	158	1595	100	37	11	Witches		—	4	29	51	13	420	78

[108   16   8   84] Supposed by me to be Middleton's additions.

HAMLET, Q 1.

Act.	Scene.	Total Lines.	Prose.	Blank.	Heroic.	Short Rhyme.	Songs.	Alternates.	Sonnets.	Doggrel.	One Measure.	Two Measure.	Three Measure.	Four Measure.	Female Ending.	Extra Syllable.
I	1	130	—	118	—	—	—	—	—	—	1	3	8	—	15	—
	2	168	—	148	2	—	—	—	—	—	2	2	11	3	36	—
	3	73	—	62	2	—	—	—	—	—	—	6	2	1	10	—
	4	61	—	55	—	—	—	—	—	—	—	1	3	2	13	—
	5	157	—	130	2	—	—	—	—	—	2	9	6	8	25	—
II	1	33	—	28	—	—	—	—	—	—	—	1	4	—	8	—
	2a	203	52	123	6	4	—	—	—	—	2	7	7	2	22	—
	2b	243	182	47	2	—	—	—	—	—	—	3	6	3	7	—
III	1	39	—	34	2	—	—	—	—	—	—	—	1	2	5	—
	2	238	162	29	2	4	[36	rhyme in play]			1	1	1	2	2	—
	3	33	—	20	6	—	—	—	—	—	1	1	2	3	2	—
	4	100	—	81	6	—	—	—	—	—	1	2	5	5	12	—
IV	1, 3	64	28	28	4	—	—	—	—	—	—	2	2	—	11	—
	4	5	—	5	—	—	—	—	—	—	—	—	—	—	3	—
	5	127	32	55	10	26	—	—	—	—	—	1	2	1	6	—
	6	36	—	31	2	—	—	—	—	—	1	2	—	—	8	—
	7	55	—	47	2	—	—	—	—	—	—	2	3	1	7	—
V	1	178	116	45	2	8	—	—	—	—	—	2	4	1	4	—
	2	125	37	69	4	1	—	—	—	—	2	—	9	3	13	—
		2068	609	1155	54	43	[36	rhyme in play]			13	45	76	37	209	—

HAMLET. [Written (perhaps with a coadjutor) 1588: revised and altered 1599: rewritten as in Q 2 1604. Q 1 is a surreptitious copy of the 1599 eked out with the 1588 version. F is an abridgement subsequent to Q 2. Query after 1616.]

Act.	Scene.	Total Lines.	Prose.	Blank.	Heroic.	Short Rhyme.	Songs.	Alternates.	Sonnets.	Doggrel.	One Measure.	Two Measure.	Three Measure.	Four Measure.	Female Ending.	Extra Syllable.
I	1	175	—	163	—	—	—	—	—	—	2	6	2	2	29	3
	2	258	—	240	8	—	—	—	—	—	2	1	6	1	60	16
	3	136	—	127	2	—	—	—	—	—	1	1	3	2	35	3
	4	91	—	87	—	—	—	—	—	—	—	1	3	—	22	—
	5	190	—	173	2	—	—	—	—	—	5	3	7	—	32	2
II	1	119	—	109	2	—	—	—	—	—	2	3	1	2	37	4
	2	634	355	255	6	—	4	—	—	—	5	4	5	—	53	3
III	1	196	68	112	6	—	—	—	—	—	—	3	4	3	35	5
	2	417	280	43	4	8	—	[81 rhyme in play]			—	1	—	—	13	2
	3	98	—	89	6	—	—	—	—	—	1	1	—	1	11	4
	4	217	—	203	6	—	—	—	—	—	—	4	4	—	29	9
IV	1	45	—	39	2	—	—	—	—	—	—	1	3	—	4	1
	2	33	33	—	—	—	—	—	—	—	—	—	—	—	—	—
	3	70	30	38	2	—	—	—	—	—	—	—	—	—	5	2
	4	66	—	62	2	—	—	—	—	—	—	1	1	—	9	2
	5	219	48	102	6	—	42	—	—	—	1	7	13	—	29	3
	6	34	8	25	—	—	—	—	—	—	—	—	1	—	1	1
	7	195	—	186	—	—	—	—	—	—	4	2	3	—	46	12
V	1	322	224	69	8	—	14	—	—	—	—	3	3	1	11	2
	2	414	154	236	2	—	—	—	—	—	2	11	7	2	67	4
		3929	1200	2358	64	8	60	[81 rhyme in play]			25	53	66	14	528	78

OTHELLO. [c. 1604.]

Act.	Scene.	Total Lines.	Prose.	Blank.	Heroic.	Short Rhyme.	Songs.	Alternates.	Sonnets.	Doggrel.	One Measure.	Two Measure.	Three Measure.	Four Measure.	Female Ending.	Extra Syllable.
I	1	184	11	159	—	—	—	—	—	—	4	5	4	1	54	14
	2	99	—	92	4	—	—	—	—	—	—	2	1		38	9
	3	410	96	276	24	—	—	—	—	—	—	7	6	1	83	24
II	1	321	110	173	24	—	—	—	—	—	3	5	6	—	41	10
	2	13	13	—	—	—	—	—	—	—	—	—	—	—	—	—
	3	394	173	191	8	—	13	—	—	—	3	3	3	—	58	12
III	1	59	29	30	—	—	—	—	—	—	—	—	—	—	14	3
	2	6	—	6	—	—	—	—	—	—	—	—	—	—	2	1
	3	478	—	435	6	—	—	—	—	—	3	15	15	4	116	42
	4	201	22	169	—	—	—	—	—	—	2	5	1	2	50	11
IV	1	293	115	169	—	—	—	—	—	—	2	3	2	2	48	13
	2	252	81	159	—	—	—	—	—	—	2	3	7	—	43	16
	3	106	11	73	4	—	12	—	—	—	1	4	1	—	20	6
V	1	129	—	109	4	—	—	—	—	—	2	4	10	—	39	13
	2	371	—	340	4	—	—	—	—	—	3	11	13	—	73	34
		3316	661	2381	78	—	25	—	—	—	25	67	69	10	679	208

KING LEAR. [Written 1605. Q is a surreptitious copy of a *revision* of the original, played at Court, December, 1606. F is a subsequent *abridgement* of the original (not of Q) made for stage purposes. Query after 1613.]

Act.	Scene.	Total Lines.	Prose.	Blank.	Heroic.	Short Rhyme.	Songs.	Alternates.	Sonnets.	Doggrel.	One Measure.	Two Measure.	Three Measure.	Four Measure.	Female Ending.	Extra Syllable.
I	1	312	61	211	26	—	—	—	—	—	3	—	10	1	63	21
	2	200	167	28	2	—	—	—	—	—	—	—	2	1	9	3
	3	26	—	21	2	—	—	—	—	—	1	—	2	—	10	3
	4	371	195	126	2	—	31	—	—	—	1	2	12	2	32	8
	5	55	50	3	—	—	—	—	—	2	—	—	—	—	—	—
II	1	131	15	110	—	—	—	—	—	—	—	—	4	2	36	6
	2	180	78	88	—	—	—	—	—	—	—	4	10	—	27	7
	3	21	—	18	2	—	—	—	—	—	—	—	1	—	1	1
	4	312	31	253	—	—	14	—	—	—	2	2	8	2	78	16
III	1	55	—	49	—	—	—	—	—	—	—	2	4	—	14	1
	2	95	11	54	—	—	26	—	—	—	—	—	3	1	16	3
	3	26	21	3	2	—	—	—	—	—	—	—	—	—	1	1
	4	188	83	87	—	—	10	—	—	—	—	4	4	—	17	3
	5	26	26	—	—	—	—	—	—	—	—	—	—	—	—	—
	6	122	57	35	12	—	16	—	—	—	—	1	1	—	10	3
	7	107	14	80	—	—	—	—	—	—	2	—	8	3	24	6
IV	1	82	9	66	—	—	—	—	—	—	1	3	3	—	12	2
	2	98	—	92	—	—	—	—	—	—	1	3	1	1	27	8
	3	57	11	43	—	—	—	—	—	—	—	1	1	1	13	2
	4	27	—	22	2	—	—	—	—	—	—	2	1	—	6	—
	5	40	—	35	—	—	—	—	—	—	2	2	1	—	10	4
	6	293	49	217	2	—	—	—	—	—	1	3	18	3	47	17
	7	98	10	75	2	—	—	—	—	—	—	5	4	2	20	5
V	1	69	—	61	2	—	—	—	—	—	1	—	5	—	21	3
	2	11	—	11	—	—	—	—	—	—	—	—	—	—	1	—
	3	326	8	284	14	—	—	—	—	—	—	3	17	—	79	8
		3328	896	2072	70	—	97	—	—	2	15	37	120	19	580	131

Act.	Scene.	Total Lines.	Prose.	Blank.	Heroic.	Short Rhyme.	Songs.	Alternates.	Sonnets.	Doggrel.	One Measure.	Two Measure.	Three Measure.	Four Measure.	Female Ending.	Extra Syllable.
I	1	62	—	60	—	—	—	—	—	—	—	—	2	—	9	2
	2	203	104	91	4	—	—	—	—	—	2	—	1	1	17	4
	3	105	—	95	6	—	—	—	—	—	1	2	1	—	29	5
	4	84	—	79	2	—	—	—	—	—	—	1	1	1	23	6
	5	77	—	71	2	—	—	—	—	—	—	—	4	—	24	4
II	1	52	—	49	2	—	—	—	—	—	1	—	—	—	14	4
	2	250	32	207	—	—	—	—	—	—	—	2	7	2	66	15
	3	42	—	39	—	—	—	—	—	—	1	—	2	—	10	2
	4	10	—	10	—	—	—	—	—	—	—	—	—	—	3	1
	5	119	—	114	—	—	—	—	—	—	—	2	2	1	34	7
	6	145	62	80	—	—	—	—	—	—	—	—	3	—	23	1
	7	142	47	79	2	—	6	—	—	—	1	2	4	1	20	3
III	1	37	—	36	—	—	—	—	—	—	—	—	1	—	14	3
	2	65	—	58	—	—	—	—	—	—	—	3	2	2	20	2
	3	51	—	49	—	—	—	—	—	—	—	1	1	—	14	2
	4	38	—	35	—	—	—	—	—	—	—	2	1	—	13	1
	5	24	11	13	—	—	—	—	—	—	—	—	—	—	3	1
	6	98	—	95	—	—	—	—	—	—	—	1	1	1	28	4
	7	82	—	81	—	—	—	—	—	—	—	1	—	—	17	3
	8	5	—	3	—	—	—	—	—	—	—	2	—	—	1	—
	9	4	—	3	—	—	—	—	—	—	—	—	1	—	—	—
	10	37	—	34	—	—	—	—	—	—	—	—	2	1	13	—
	11	74	—	68	2	—	—	—	—	—	—	—	3	1	5	4
	12	36	—	36	—	—	—	—	—	—	—	—	—	—	8	—
	13	201	—	188	2	—	—	—	—	—	1	2	3	5	37	11
IV	1	16	—	16	—	—	—	—	—	—	—	—	—	—	4	3
	2	45	—	42	—	—	—	—	—	—	—	1	1	1	9	—
	3	23	—	22	—	—	—	—	—	—	—	1	—	—	5	—
	4	38	—	34	2	—	—	—	—	—	—	—	1	1	6	—
	5	17	—	17	—	—	—	—	—	—	—	—	—	—	8	—
	6	39	—	35	—	—	—	—	—	—	—	2	1	1	7	1
	7	16	—	14	—	—	—	—	—	—	—	—	2	—	3	1
	8	39	—	35	2	—	—	—	—	—	—	—	1	1	5	—
	9	34	—	33	—	—	—	—	—	—	—	—	—	1	6	2
	10	9	—	8	—	—	—	—	—	—	—	—	1	—	2	—
	11	4	—	3	—	—	—	—	—	—	—	—	1	—	—	—
	12	49	—	48	—	—	—	—	—	—	—	—	1	—	7	—
	13	10	—	10	—	—	—	—	—	—	—	—	—	—	4	—
	14	140	—	130	2	—	—	—	—	—	—	2	6	—	29	11
	15	91	—	84	2	—	—	—	—	—	—	1	2	2	23	—
V	1	77	—	73	—	—	—	—	—	—	—	—	2	2	22	3
	2	369	31	312	4	—	—	—	—	—	4	7	10	1	81	14
		3059	287	2589	34	—	6	—	—	—	11	35	71	26	666	120

CORIOLANUS. [1608.]

Act.	Scene.	Total Lines.	Prose.	Blank.	Heroic.	Short Rhyme.	Songs.	Alternates.	Sonnets.	Doggrel.	One Measure.	Two Measure.	Three Measure.	Four Measure.	Female Ending.	Extra Syllable.
I	1	283	76	196	—	—	—	—	—	—	—	2	8	1	81	9
	2	37	—	36	—	—	—	—	—	—	—	—	—	1	11	2
	3	124	100	21	—	—	—	—	—	—	—	—	3	—	5	1
	4	62	—	61	—	—	—	—	—	—	—	—	1	—	17	5
	5	29	—	27	—	—	—	—	—	—	—	1	—	1	5	1
	6	87	—	81	—	—	—	—	—	—	—	1	4	1	26	2
	7	7	—	6	—	—	—	—	—	—	—	—	1	—	1	—
	8	15	—	13	—	—	—	—	—	—	—	—	2	—	5	3
	9	94	—	92	—	—	—	—	—	—	—	—	2	—	27	3
	10	33	—	33	—	—	—	—	—	—	—	—	—	—	14	2
II	1	286	176	100	6	—	—	—	—	—	—	—	3	1	33	4
	2	164	40	121	—	—	—	—	—	—	—	1	2	—	42	8
	3	271	110	143	12	—	—	—	—	—	—	1	5	—	52	10
III	1	336	—	318	—	—	—	—	—	—	—	3	11	4	87	21
	2	144	—	136	—	—	—	—	—	—	—	2	4	2	37	3
	3	143	—	131	—	—	—	—	—	—	—	1	6	5	34	6
IV	1	58	—	56	—	—	—	—	—	—	1	1	—	—	9	—
	2	54	—	50	—	—	—	—	—	—	—	3	1	—	10	2
	3	57	57	—	—	—	—	—	—	—	—	—	—	—	—	—
	4	26	—	25	—	—	—	—	—	—	—	—	1	—	4	1
	5	251	140	99	—	—	—	—	—	—	2	2	7	1	17	5
	6	161	13	132	—	—	—	—	—	—	—	5	6	5	42	6
	7	57	—	50	4	—	—	—	—	—	—	—	2	1	18	4
V	1	74	—	70	—	—	—	—	—	—	—	2	2	—	18	4
	2	117	80	33	—	—	—	—	—	—	1	1	2	—	9	1
	3	209	—	204	2	—	—	—	—	—	—	1	1	1	53	13
	4	65	37	27	—	—	—	—	—	—	—	1	—	—	8	—
	5	6	—	6	—	—	—	—	—	—	—	—	—	—	3	—
	6	156	—	146	4	—	—	—	—	—	1	2	3	—	42	4
		3406	829	2413	28	—	—	—	—	—	5	30	77	24	710	120

CYMBELINE. [Partly written c. 1606: completed 1609.]

Act	Scene	Total Lines	Prose.	Blank.	Heroic.	Short Rhyme.	Songs.	Alternates.	Sonnets.	Doggrel.	One Measure.	Two Measure.	Three Measure.	Four Measure.	Female Ending.	Extra Syllable.
I	1a	69	—	68	—	—	—	—	—	—	—	1	—	—	24	—
	1b	109	—	106	—	—	—	—	—	—	—	1	1	1	35	2
	2	43	43	—	—	—	—	—	—	—	—	—	—	—	—	—
	3	40	—	38	—	—	—	—	—	—	—	1	—	1	11	1
	4	185	185	—	—	—	—	—	—	—	—	—	—	—	—	—
	5	87	—	83	2	—	—	—	—	—	1	—	1	—	26	4
	6	210	4	197	—	—	—	—	—	—	1	3	4	1	52	1
II	1	70	56	11	2	—	—	—	—	—	—	—	—	1	4	—
	2	51	—	47	2	—	—	—	—	—	—	1	1	—	16	2
	3	161	31	116	—	—	8	—	—	—	2	—	3	1	31	5
	4	152	—	147	2	—	—	—	—	—	—	—	1	2	54	7
	5	35	—	31	2	—	—	—	—	—	—	1	—	1	10	—
III	1	87	21	62	—	—	—	—	—	—	—	—	4	—	23	3
	2	84	10	71	2	—	—	—	—	—	—	—	1	—	23	5
	3	107	—	107	—	—	—	—	—	—	—	—	—	—	25	7
	4	196	13	177	—	—	—	—	—	—	—	1	2	3	57	12
	5	168	66	88	12	—	—	—	—	—	—	—	1	1	36	2
	6	95	—	91	—		—	—	—	—	—	1	3	—	29	3
	7	16	—	16	—	—	—	—	—	—	—	—	—	—	7	1
IV	1	27	27	—	—	—	—	—	—	—	—	—	—	—	—	—
	2	403	—	340	32	—	24	—	—	—	1	2	—	4	110	17
	3	46	—	43	2	—	—	—	—	—	—	—	—	1	14	2
	4	54	—	50	4	—	—	—	—	—	—	—	—	—	19	—
V	1	33	—	29	4	—	—	—	—	—	—	—	—	—	7	—
	2	17	—	12	4	—	—	—	—	—	—	—	1	—	4	—
	3	94	—	84	10	—	—	—	—	—	—	—	—	—	28	2
	4	215	71	50	6	[63	—	23	in vision]		—	1	1	—	17	2
	5	485	8	464	4	—	—	—	—	—	—	2	6	1	137	12
		3339	535	2528	90	[63]	32	[23]	—	—	5	15	30	18	799	90

III 5 and IV 2—V 3 are earlier work than the rest.

TEMPEST. [1610: as we have it, it is greatly abridged.]

Act.	Scene.	Total Lines.	Prose.	Blank.	Heroic.	Short Rhyme.	Songs.	Alternates.	Sonnets.	Doggerel.	One Measure.	Two Measure.	Three Measure.	Four Measure.	Female Ending.	Extra Syllable.
I	1	71	57	14	[but nearly all this scene was originally verse]								—	—	6	—
	2	501	—	465	—	—	21	—	—	—	2	5	7	1	170	8
II	1	327	129	181	2	—	6	—	—	—	1	2	4	2	55	4
	2	192	128	39	—	—	18	—	—	—	—	2	5	—	14	—
III	1	96	—	93	2	—	—	—	—	—	—	—	1	—	40	2
	2	161	97	53	—	—	3	—	—	—	—	4	4	—	20	2
	3	109	—	105	—	—	—	—	—	—	—	1	3	—	40	5
IV	1	267	39	141	—	4	5	[masque 54 rhyme			—	3	9	—	39	5
V	1	318	8	289	—	—	7	12 songs]			—	3	9	2	88	7
Epilogue		20	—	—	—	20	—	—	—	—	—	—	—	—	—	—
		2062	458	1390	4	24	50	[masque 54, 12]			3	20	42	5	472	33

WINTER'S TALE. [1611.]

Act	Scene	Total Lines	Prose.	Blank.	Heroic.	Short Rhyme.	Songs.	Alternates.	Sonnets.	Doggrel.	One Measure.	Two Measure.	Three Measure	Four Measure.	Female Ending	Extra Syllable.
I	1	50	50	—	—	—	—	—	—	—	—	—	—	—	—	—
	2	465	—	459	—	—	—	—	—	—	—	1	2	3	159	23
II	1	199	—	193	—	—	—	—	—	—	—	1	4	1	60	3
	2	65	—	58	—	—	—	—	—	—	—	3	4	—	21	3
	3	207	—	198	2	—	—	—	—	—	1	1	4	1	72	5
III	1	22	—	21	—	—	—	—	—	—	—	—	1	—	11	—
	2	244	16	219	—	—	—	—	—	—	—	2	4	3	66	5
	3	143	85	56	—	—	—	—	—	—	—	2	—	—	18	3
IV	1	32	—	—	32	(Chorus)		—	—	—	—	—	—	—	—	—
	2	62	62	—	—	—	—	—	—	—	—	—	—	—	—	—
	3	135	111	—	—	—	24	—	—	—	—	—	—	—	—	—
	4	874	467	364	—	—	33	—	—	—	—	3	5	2	144	12
V	1	233	—	226	—	—	—	—	—	—	2	1	1	3	68	2
	2	188	188	—	—	—	—	—	—	—	—	—	—	—	—	—
	3	155	—	152	—	—	—	—	—	—	1	—	1	1	56	4
		3074	979	1946	34	—	57	—	—	—	4	14	26	14	675	60

JULIUS CÆSAR. [1600: as we have it the play is much abridged, about three-fourths of the length of the other Roman plays.]

Act.	Scene.	Total Lines.	Prose.	Blank.	Heroic.	Short Rhyme.	Songs.	Alternates.	Sonnets.	Doggrel.	One Measure.	Two Measure.	Three Measure.	Four Measure.	Female Ending.	Extra Syllable.
I	1	80	21	51	4	—	—	—	—	—	1	1	2	—	2	—
	2	326	56	255	2	—	—	—	—	—	2	4	7	—	41	4
	3	164	—	163	—	—	—	—	—	—	—	—	1	—	22	—
II	1	334	—	313	4	—	—	—	—	—	2	7	6	2	65	5
	2	129	—	123	2	—	—	—	—	—	1	1	1	1	21	2
	3	16	—	14	2	—	—	—	—	—	—	—	—	—	6	3
	4	46	—	42	—	—	—	—	—	—	—	—	3	1	9	—
III	1	297	—	280	—	—	—	—	—	—	2	4	10	1	56	6
	2	276	40	225	—	—	—	—	—	—	2	4	5	—	54	1
	3	43	39	4	—	—	—	—	—	—	—	—	—	—	1	—
IV	1	51	—	50	—	—	—	—	—	—	—	1	—	—	7	—
	2	52	—	51	—	—	—	—	—	—	—	—	—	1	7	1
	3	309	—	288	4	—	—	—	—	—	1	5	8	3	60	8
V	1	125	—	117	—	—	—	—	—	—	2	6	—	—	23	—
	2	6	—	6	—	—	—	—	—	—	—	—	—	—	—	—
	3	110	—	97	8	—	—	—	—	—	—	2	3	—	15	3
	4	32	—	31	—	—	—	—	—	—	1	—	—	—	4	—
	5	81	—	71	6	—	—	—	—	—	1	1	1	1	20	2
		2477	156	2181	32	—	—	—	—	—	15	36	47	10	413	35

SHAKESPEARE'S PART.

Act.	Scene.	Total Lines.	Prose.	Blank.	Heroic.	Short Rhyme.	Songs.	Alternates.	Sonnets.	Doggrel.	One Measure.	Two Measure.	Three Measure.	Four Measure.	Female Ending.	Extra Syllable.
II	1, 166-326	160	—	153	2	—	—	—	—	—	—	1	2	2	31	1
III	2, 151-241	91	—	86	2	—	—	—	—	—	—	—	—	3	8	2
IV	1	224	122	97	2	—	—	—	—	—	—	1	—	2	30	1
	3	198	—	182	8	—	—	—	—	—	—	2	4	2	23	2
	5	79	—	77	2	—	—	—	—	—	—	—	—	—	18	1
V	2, 1-179	179	—	155	12	—	—	—	—	—	1	8	3	—	36	4
		931	122	750	28	—	—	—	—	—	1	12	9	9	146	11

INDUCTION.

Act.	Scene.	Total Lines.	Prose.	Blank.	Heroic.	Short Rhyme.	Songs.	Alternates.	Sonnets.	Doggrel.	One Measure.	Two Measure.	Three Measure.	Four Measure.	Female Ending.	Extra Syllable.
	1	138	15	120	—	—	—	—	—	—	—	2	—	1	26	—
	2	147	24	120	—	—	—	—	—	—	1	—	2	—	15	2
		285	39	240	—	—	—	—	—	—	1	2	2	1	41	2

SECOND AUTHOR.

Act.	Scene.	Total Lines.	Prose.	Blank.	Heroic.	Short Rhyme.	Songs.	Alternates.	Sonnets.	Doggrel.	One Measure.	Two Measure.	Three Measure.	Four Measure.	Female Ending.	Extra Syllable.
I	1	253	49	180	8	—	—	—	—	8	—	2	1	1	25	—
	2	282	39	195	14	—	—	—	—	27	1	1	4	1	38	1
II	1, 1-165	165	9	151	—	—	—	—	—	2	—	2	1	—	32	1
II	1, 327-413	87	—	72	10	—	—	—	—	2	—	1	2	—	16	1
III	1	92	20	60	6	—	—	6	—	—	—	—	—	—	3	—
III	2, 1-150	150	54	86	4	5	—	—	—	—	—	—	1	—	13	1
III	2, 242-254	13	—	11	2	—	—	—	—	—	—	—	—	—	4	—
IV	2	120	—	113	6	—	—	—	—	—	—	1	—	—	32	2
	4	109	29	68	2	2	—	—	—	2	1	1	—	4	19	1
V	1	155	123	16	10	—	—	—	—	6	—	—	—	—	2	—
	2, 180-189	10	—	—	2	—	—	—	—	8	—	—	—	—	—	—
		1436	323	958	64	7	—	6	—	53	2	8	9	6	184	7

INDUCTION AFTER I 1.

Act.	Scene.	Total Lines.	Prose.	Blank.	Heroic.	Short Rhyme.	Songs.	Alternates.	Sonnets.	Doggrel.	One Measure.	Two Measure.	Three Measure.	Four Measure.	Female Ending.	Extra Syllable.
		4	—	—	2	—	—	—	—	2	—	—	—	—	—	—

N.B.—Some of Grumio's *prose* in I 2 is of Shakespeare's insertion. IV 5, 76-79 are spurious, and the Hortensio of IV 3 and IV 5 is in my opinion a late stage alteration. He was originally Petruchio's cousin Ferdinand, not the wooer of Bianca.

TROYLUS AND CRESSIDA. [Troylus story by Shakespeare c. 1594: play completed by another hand 1599: revised 1602: Ajax story rewritten by Shakespeare c. 1605, ending at V 3.

TROYLUS STORY (TIME OF WAR).

Act.	Scene.	Total Lines.	Prose.	Blank.	Heroic.	Short Rhyme.	Songs.	Alternates.	Sonnets.	Doggrel.	One Measure.	Two Measure.	Three Measure.	Four Measure.	Female Ending.	Extra Syllable.
I	1	119	44	67	8	—	—	—	—	—	—	—	—	—	11	—
	2	321	269	38	14	—	—	—	—	—	—	—	—	—	3	—
III	1	171	148	11	—	—	12	—	—	—	—	—	—	—	4	3
	2	220	107	99	6	—	—	—	—	—	—	4	4	—	17	1
IV	1	79	—	67	8	—	—	—	—	—	—	2	2	—	17	3
	2	115	32	76	—	—	—	—	—	—	2	1	4	—	18	5
	3	12	—	10	—	—	—	—	—	—	—	—	2	—	2	—
	4	150	12	111	12	4	—	—	—	—	—	2	8	1	31	5
	5, 12-63	52	—	26	22	—	—	—	—	—	—	2	2	—	6	—
V	2	197	15	154	10	—	—	—	—	—	3	5	9	1	33	7
	3	21	11	5	4	—	—	—	—	—	—	1	—	—	1	—
		1457	638	664	84	4	12	—	—	—	5	17	31	2	143	24

The (prose) Thersites part of V 2 was clearly added in the revision c. 1605. III 3, 1-33: IV 5, 277-293: V 1, 87-95, must have had equivalents in, if they are not fragments of, the 1599 version.

AJAX STORY (TIME OF TRUCE).

Act.	Scene.	Total Lines.	Prose.	Blank.	Heroic.	Short Rhyme.	Songs.	Alternates.	Sonnets.	Doggrel.	One Measure.	Two Measure.	Three Measure.	Four Measure.	Female Ending.	Extra Syllable.
II	1	142	132	10	—	—	—	—	—	—	—	—	—	—	—	—
	2	213	—	195	12	—	—	—	—	—	—	2	4	—	45	10
	3	277	143	125	4	—	—	—	—	—	—	2	1	2	32	12
III	3	316	70	232	6	—	—	—	—	—	—	4	3	1	66	14
IV	5, except 12-53	241	—	221	10	—	—	—	—	—	—	6	3	1	55	15
V	1	106	69	30	4	—	—	—	—	—	—	1	2	—	5	2
	3, 1-94	94	—	83	6	—	—	—	—	—	—	3	2	—	19	5
		1389	414	896	42	—	—	—	—	—	—	18	15	4	222	58

REMNANT OF 1599 PLAY, BY THE SECOND HAND CHIEFLY.

Act.	Scene.	Total Lines.	Prose.	Blank.	Heroic.	Short Rhyme.	Songs.	Alternates.	Sonnets.	Doggrel.	One Measure.	Two Measure.	Three Measure.	Four Measure.	Female Ending.	Extra Syllable.
	Prologue	31	—	25	4	—	—	—	—	—	—	—	2	—	5	2
V	4	38	30	5	—	—	—	—	—	—	1	—	2	—	—	1
	5	45	—	42	—	—	—	—	—	—	—	2	1	—	15	2
	6	31	—	24	4	—	—	—	—	—	—	3	—	—	7	2
	7	24	16	6	2	—	—	—	—	—	—	—	—	—	—	—
	8	22	—	8	14	—	—	—	—	—	—	—	—	—	—	—
	9	10	—	4	6	—	—	—	—	—	—	—	—	—	3	—
	10	57	10	27	20	—	—	—	—	—	—	—	—	—	1	—

Act	Scene	Total Lines	Prose	Blank	Heroic	Short Rhyme	Songs	Alternates	Sonnets	Doggrel	One Measure	Two Measure	Three Measure	Four Measure	Female Ending	Extra Syllable
I	1, 1-182	182	—	164	2	—	—	—	—	—	3	5	5	3	54	8
	249-264	16	—	14	—	—	—	—	—	—	—	—	2	—		1
	234-295	12	—	9	—	—	—	—	—	—	—	—	3	—	1	2
II	1	35	—	33	—		—	—	—	—	1		—	1	8	4
	2, 1-44	44	—	39	2	—	—	—	—	—	—	2	—	1	11	3
	132-194	63	—	61	—	—	—	—	—	—	—	1	—	1	13	
	205-242	38	—	34	4		—	—	—	—	—				15	3
III	6, 98-115	18	—	13	4	—	—	—	—	—	—	—	—	1	2	
IV	1	40	—	34	6	—	—	—	—	—	—	—	—		4	—
	2, 1-29	29	—	27	2	—	—	—	—	—		—	—	—	2	
	3, 1-291	291	—	273	—	—	—	—	—	—	3	5	7	3	63	16
	303-398	26	—	24	2	—	—	—	—	—	—	—	—	—	4	—
	415-453	37		36	—	—	—	—		—		—	1	—	5	—
V	1, 58-231	174	—	161	4	—	—	—		—		3	5	1	49	5
	2	17	—	14	2	—	—	—	—	—	—	1	—	—	6	
	4	85		74	4	4 ballad from North]				—	—	1	2		6	2
		1107		1010	32	[4	—	—	—	—	7	18	25	11	243	44
SECOND HAND.																
I	1, 183-248	66	66	—	—	—	—	—	—	—	—	—	—	—		
	265-283	17	17	—	—	—	—	—	—	—	—	—	—	—		
	2	257	96	100	36	10	—	—	—	—	1	2	8	4	33	
II	2, 45-131	87	87	—	—	—	—	—	—	—	—	—	—	—	—	
	195-204	10	10	—	—	—	—	—	—	—		—	—	—	—	
III	1	66	49	13	2	—	—	—	—	—	—	—	2		5	
	2	94	58	32	4	—	—	—	—	—	—	—	—	—	3	
	3	42	8	25	6	—	—	—	—	—	—	1	2	—	10	
	4	118	18	81	8	—	—	—	—	—	—	7	4	—	9	2
	5	117	—	79	28		—	—	—	—	2	2	5	1	16	
	6, 1-97	97	97	—		—	—	—	—	—	—	—	—	—	—	
	116-131	16	14	—	2	—	—	—	—	—	—	—	—	—	—	
IV	2, 30-50	21	—	11	8	—	—	—	—		—	—	1	1	3	1
	3, 292-362	71	71	—	—	—	—	—	—	—	—	—	—	—	—	
	399-414	16	16	—	—	—	—	—	—	—	—					
	453-543	91	12	54	16	—	—	—	—	—	—	6	2	1	10	3
V	1, 1-58	58	41	9	6	—	—	—	—		—	2	—		2	—
	3	10	—	6	4	—	—	—	—	—	—	—	—		—	—
		1254	600	410	120	10	—	—	—	—	3	20	24	7	91	6

III 3, 70-75: 103-106, are also probably inserted by the second hand.

PERICLES. [1606.]

SHAKESPEARE'S PART.

Act.	Scene.	Total Lines.	Prose.	Blank.	Heroic.	Short Rhyme.	Songs.	Alternates.	Sonnets.	Doggrel.	One Measure.	Two Measure.	Three Measure.	Four Measure.	Female Ending.	Extra Syllable.
III	1	82	—	79	—	—	—	—	—	—	—	2	1	—	17	5
	2	111	—	90	—	8	—	—	—	—	—	2	9	2	23	4
	3	41	—	40	—	—	—	—	—	—	—	—	1	—	9	—
	4	18	—	14	2	—	—	—	—	—	—	1	1	—	3	—
IV	1	103	—	95	2	—	—	—	—	—	—	—	4	2	19	2
	3	51	—	44	2	—	—	—	—	—	—	1	4	—	13	1
V	1	266	—	232	2	—	—	[8 vision?]		—	2	7	10	5	55	13
	3	84	—	68	6	—	—	—	—	—	1	4	4	1	17	3
		756	—	662	14	8	—	[8]	—	—	3	17	34	10	156	28

THE PLOTTER'S PART.

Act.	Scene.	Total Lines.	Prose.	Blank.	Heroic.	Short Rhyme.	Songs.	Alternates.	Sonnets.	Doggrel.	One Measure.	Two Measure.	Three Measure.	Four Measure.	Female Ending.	Extra Syllable.
Gower 1		42	—	—	7	35	—	—	—	—	—	—	—	—	—	—
I	1	171	—	118	46	—	—	—	—	—	2	1	4	—	10	—
	2	124	—	99	20	—	—	—	—	—	—	—	4	1	23	—
	3	40	10	25	2	—	—	—	—	—	—	2	1	—	7	—
	4	108	—	69	29	—	—	—	—	—	—	8	2	—	9	—
Gower 2		40	—	—	1	39	—	—	—	—	—	—	—	—	—	—
II	1	172	92	66	12	—	—	—	—	—	—	1	1	—	11	—
	2	59	—	45	12	—	—	—	—	—	1	1	—	—	6	—
	3	116	—	82	28	—	—	—	—	—	2	—	3	1	13	—
	4	58	—	41	14	—	—	—	—	—	—	1	1	1	5	—
	5	93	—	79	12	—	—	—	—	—	1	1	—	—	7	—
Gower 3		60	—	—	—	60	—	—	—	—	—	—	—	—	—	—
Gower 4		52	—	—	1	51	—	—	—	—	—	—	—	—	—	—
		1135	102	624	184	185	—	—	—	—	6	15	16	3	91	—

THIRD HAND.

TWO NOBLE KINSMEN. [1612.]

SHAKESPEARE'S PART.

Act.	Scene.	Total Lines.	Prose.	Blank.	Heroic.	Short Rhyme.	Songs.	Alternates.	Sonnets.	Doggrel.	One Measure.	Two Measure.	Three Measure.	Four Measure.	Female Ending.	Extra Syllable.
I	1	233	—	200	—	—	24	—	—	—	—	4	5	—	51	4
	2	116	—	114			—	—	—	—	—	—	2	—	37	7
	3	100	—	98	—		—		—	—	1	—	1	—	37	3
	4	49	—	47	—	—	—	—	—	—	—	1	1	—	12	2
	5	15	—	2	4	—	9	—	—	—	—	—	—	—	—	—
II	1a	67	67		—	—	—	—	—	—	—	—	—	—	—	—
III	1	122	—	121	—	—	—	—	—	—	—	—	1	—	36	1
	2	38	—	37	—	—	—	—	—	—	—	—	1	—	9	1
IV	3	112	112	—	—	—	—	—	—	—	—		—			
V	1	173	—	165	—	—	—	—	—	—	—	2	6	—	50	4
	3	146	—	140	—		—	—	—	—	—	3	3	—	42	3
	4	147	—	144	—	—	—	—	—	—	—	1	1	1	47	5
		1318	179	1068	4	—	33	—	—	—	1	11	21	1	321	30

FLETCHER'S PART.

Act.	Scene.	Total Lines.	Prose.	Blank.	Heroic.	Short Rhyme.	Songs.	Alternates.	Sonnets.	Doggrel.	One Measure.	Two Measure.	Three Measure.	Four Measure.	Female Ending.	Extra Syllable.
II	1b	275	—	273	—	—	—	—	—	—	—	—	1	1	158	2
	2	82	—	77	—	—	—	—	—	—	1	—	1	3	38	1
	3	33	—	31	—	—		—	—	—		—	—	2	18	
	4	64	—	62	—	—		—	—		1	—	—	1	45	—
	5	39	—	39	—			—	—		—	—	—	—	23	—
III	3	53	—	53	—	—		—	—	—	—	—	—	—	32	
	4	26	—	20	—	—	6	—	—	—	—	—	—	—	11	—
	5	144	—	71	36	14	12	—	—	—	1	2	6	2	51	—
	6	308	—	300	2	—	—	—	—	—	1	1	1	3	192	1
IV	1	150	—	143	—	—	—	—	—	—	—	1	2	4	61	
	2	156	—	152	2	—	—	—	—	—	—	—	—	2	78	—
V	2	111	—	105	—	—	—	—	—	—	—	2	3	1	64	—
		1441	—	1326	40	14	18	—	—	—	4	6	14	19	771	4

HENRY VIII. [1613.]

SHAKESPEARE'S PART.

Act.	Scene.	Total Lines.	Prose.	Blank.	Heroic.	Short Rhyme.	Songs.	Alternates.	Sonnets.	Doggrel.	One Measure.	Two Measure.	Three Measure.	Four Measure.	Female Ending.	Extra Syllable.
I	1	226	—	221	2	—	—	—	—	—	—	—	3	—	63	7
	2	214	—	210	—	—	—	—	—	—		—	3	1	73	5
II	3	107	—	103	2	—	—	—	—	—	—	1	1	—	41	1
	4	241	—	238	—	—	—		—		—	1	1	1	72	6
III	2a	203	—	195	2	—	—	—	—		—	4	—	2	63	7
V	1	178	—	171	—	—	—	—	—	—	—	3	2	2	62	8
		1169	—	1138	6	—	—	—		—	—	9	10	6	374	34

FLETCHER'S PART.

Act.	Scene.	Total Lines.	Prose.	Blank.	Heroic.	Short Rhyme.	Songs.	Alternates.	Sonnets.	Doggrel.	One Measure.	Two Measure.	Three Measure.	Four Measure.	Female Ending.	Extra Syllable.
Prologue		32	—		32	—	—	—	—	—					—	
I	3	67	—	67	—	—		—	—	—	—	—	—	—	46	—
	4	107	—	103	—	—	—	—	—	—	—	3	1		60	—
II	1	169	—	160	—	—	—	—	—	—	1	1	1	—	93	—
	2	144	—	138	—	—	—	—	—	—	—	2	3	1	82	—
III	1	184	—	169	2	—	12	—	—	—	—	—	1	—	108	—
	2b	257	—	254	2	—	—	—	—	—	—	—	1	—	152	1
IV	1	117	—	115	—	—	—	—	—	—	—	1	1	—	54	—
	2	173	—	172	—	—	—	—	—	—	—	1	—	—	90	—
V	2	35	—	33	—	—	—	—	—	—	—	—	1	1	17	—
	3	182	—	180	2	—	—	—	—	—	—	—	—	—	97	—
	4	95	—	85	—	—	—	—	—	—	1	3	6	—	43	2
	5	77	?4	71	2	—	—	—	—	—	—	—	—	—	44	—
Epilogue		14	—	—	14	—	—	—		—	—	—	—	—		—
		1653	?4	1553	54	—	12	—	—	—	2	11	15	2	892	3

UN-SHAKESPEARIAN PART.

Act.	Scene.	Total Lines.	Prose.	Blank.	Heroic.	Short Rhyme.	Songs.	Alternates.	Sonnets.	Doggrel.	One Measure.	Two Measure.	Three Measure.	Four Measure.	Female Ending.	Extra Syllable.
I	1	177	—	161	16	—	—	—	—	—	—	—	—	—	10	—
	2	150	—	133	16	—	—	—	—	—	1	—	—	—	9	1
	3	91	—	81	10	—	—	—	—	—	—	—	—	—	10	—
	4	111	—	109	—	—	—	—	—	—	—	1	—	1	12	—
	5	39	—	39	—	—	—	—	—	—	—	—	—	—	6	—
	6	31	—	28	2	—	—	—	—	—	—	—	—	1	5	—
II	1	81	—	79	2	—	—	—	—	—	—	—	—	—	3	1
	2	60	—	58	2	—	—	—	—	—	—	—	—	—	3	—
	3	82	—	80	—	—	—	—	—	—	—	—	1	1	7	—
III	1	201	—	197	2	—	—	—	—	—	—	1	—	1	8	—
	2	137	—	128	6	—	—	—	—	—	—	3	—	—	6	—
	3	91	—	89	2	—	—	—	—	—	—	—	—	—	3	—
	4	45	—	45	—	—	—	—	—	—	—	—	—	—	—	—
IV	1	194	—	186	8	—	—	—	—	—	—	—	—	—	12	—
V	1	62	—	58	4	—	—	—	—	—	—	—	—	—	6	—
	3a	44	—	44	—	—	—	—	—	—	—	—	—	—	—	—
	3b	151	—	136	12	—	—	—	—	—	—	—	—	3	7	—
	4a	33	—	33	—	—	—	—	—	—	—	—	—	—	—	—
	4b	142	—	139	2	—	—	—	—	—	1	—	—	—	14	—
	5	108	—	106	2	—	—	—	—	—	—	—	—	—	—	—
		2030	—	1929	86	—	—	—	—	—	2	5	1	7	121	2

SHAKESPEARE'S PART, 1592.

Act.	Scene.	Total Lines.	Prose.	Blank.	Heroic.	Short Rhyme.	Songs.	Alternates.	Sonnets.	Doggrel.	One Measure.	Two Measure.	Three Measure.	Four Measure.	Female Ending.	Extra Syllable.
IV	2	56	—	52	4	—	—	—	—	—	—	—	—	—	8	—
	3	53	—	33	20	—	—	—	—	—	—	—	—	—	8	—
	4	46	—	38	8	—	—	—	—	—	—	—	—	—	11	—
	5	55	—	13	42	—	—	—	—	—	—	—	—	—	2	—
	6	57	—	1	56	—	—	—	—	—	—	—	—	—	—	—
	7	96	—	37	56	—	—	—	—	—	1	—	1	1	5	1
V	2	21	—	15	6	—	—	—	—	—	—	—	—	—	—	—
		384	—	189	192	—	—	—	—	—	1	—	1	1	34	1

SHAKESPEARE'S ADDITIONS, c. 1600.

Act.	Scene.	Total Lines.	Prose.	Blank.	Heroic.	Short Rhyme.	Songs.	Alternates.	Sonnets.	Doggrel.	One Measure.	Two Measure.	Three Measure.	Four Measure.	Female Ending.	Extra Syllable.
II	4	134	—	119	12	—	—	—	—	—	1	—	1	1	32	—
	5	129	—	119	10	—	—	—	—	—	—	—	—	—	4	—
		263	—	238	22	—	—	—	—	—	1	—	1	1	36	—

2 HENRY VI. [Written by Marlow and Greene (not Peele, as I once thought) c. 1590: revised and enlarged by Marlow nearly as in Folio 1592-3. The Quarto is a surreptitious copy of F from shorthand notes supplemented from the 1590 version: slightly revised by Shakespeare as in F c. 1601.]

Act.	Scene.	Total Lines.	Prose.	Blank.	Heroic.	Short Rhyme.	Songs.	Alternates.	Sonnets.	Doggrel.	One Measure.	Two Measure.	Three Measure.	Four Measure.	Female Ending.	Extra Syllable.
I	1	259	—	251	4	—	—	—	—	—	2	1	1	—	24	—
	2	107	—	100	6	—	—	—	—	—	—	1	—	—	14	—
	3	226	57	164	2	—	—	—	—	—	—	2	1	—	18	2
	4	84	17	59	—	—	—	—	—	—	—	6	1	1	7	—
II	1	205	—	181	16	—	—	—	—	—	1	2	4	1	27	3
	2	82	—	81	—	—	—	—	—	—	1	—	—	—	10	1
	3	108	33	65	10	—	—	—	—	—	—	—	—	—	7	1
	4	110	—	109	—	—	—	—	—	—	—	—	1	—	12	—
III	1	383	—	366	16	—	—	—	—	—	—	1	—	—	58	1
	2	412	—	403	4	—	—	—	—	—	—	1	3	1	58	—
	3	33	—	31	2	—	—	—	—	—	—	—	—	—	6	—
IV	1	147	—	144	2	—	—	—	—	—	—	—	—	1	15	—
	2	200	156	37	4	—	—	—	—	—	2	—	1	—	1	—
	3	20	20	—	—	—	—	—	—	—	—	—	—	—	—	—
	4	60	—	53	4	—	—	—	—	—	—	1	1	1	4	—
	5	13	6	7	—	—	—	—	—	—	—	—	—	—	—	—
	6	18	18	—	—	—	—	—	—	—	—	—	—	—	—	—
	7	145	105	38	2	—	—	—	—	—	—	—	—	—	6	—
	8	72	32	34	6	—	—	—	—	—	—	—	—	—	6	—
	9	49	—	46	—	—	—	—	—	—	1	—	—	2	12	—
	10	90	48	38	4	—	—	—	—	—	—	—	—	—	9	—
V	1	216	—	207	4	—	—	—	—	—	1	1	—	3	23	1
	2a	30	—	28	2	—	—	—	—	—	—	—	—	—	3	—
	2b	35	—	33	—	—	—	—	—	—	—	—	1	1	3	2
	2c	6	—	3	2	—	—	—	—	—	—	1	—	—	—	—
	2d	19	—	13	4	—	—	—	—	—	—	—	—	2	3	1
	3	33	—	31	2	—	—	—	—	—	—	—	—	—	6	1
		3162	492	2522	96	—	—	—	—	—	8	17	14	13	332	13

3 HENRY VI. [Written by Marlow and Peele 1592: revised and enlarged by Peele for Pembroke's players 1593-4, nearly as in Folio. The Octavo is a surreptitious copy taken from shorthand notes and supplemented for the 1592 version. Slightly revised by Shakespeare as in F c. 1601.]

Act.	Scene.	Total Lines.	Prose.	Blank	Heroic	Short Rhyme.	Songs.	Alternates.	Sonnets.	Doggrel.	One Measure.	Two Measure.	Three Measure	Four Measure.	Female Ending.	Extra Syllable
I	1	273	—	264	6	—	—	—	—	—	3	—	—	—	20	2
	2	76	—	70	4	—	—	—	—	—	1	—	1	—	7	—
	3	52	—	47	2	—	—	—	—	—	2	—	1	—	3	—
	4	180	—	176	4	—	—	—	—	—	—	—	—	—	23	1
II	1	209	—	203	6	—	—	—	—	—	—	—	—	—	18	—
	2	177	—	169	6	—	—	—	—	—	—	2	—	—	9	1
	3	56	—	54	2	—	—	—	—	—	—	—	—	—	3	—
	4	13	—	12	—	—	—	—	—	—	—	1	—	—	2	—
	5	139	—	131	8	—	—	—	—	—	—	—	—	—	12	—
	6	110	—	108	2	—	—	—	—	—	—	—	—	—	12	—
III	1	101	—	100	—	—	—	—	—	—	1	—	—	—	15	—
	2	195	—	184	8	—	—	—	—	—	1	1	1	—	30	1
	3	265	—	246	10	—	—	—	—	—	—	1	2	—	45	1
IV	1	149	—	138	7	—	—	—	—	—	1	1	2	—	37	—
	2	29	—	28	—	—	—	—	—	—	—	—	1	—	9	1
	3	64	—	58	4	—	—	—	—	—	—	—	1	1	10	1
	4	35	—	27	7	—	—	—	—	—	—	—	1	—	6	—
	5	29	—	20	2	—	—	—	—	—	—	—	1	—	4	—
	6	102	—	81	20	—	—	—	—	—	—	1	—	—	17	—
	7	88	—	81	6	—	—	—	—	—	—	—	1	—	20	1
	8	84	—	78	4	—	—	—	—	—	—	1	—	1	4	—
V	1	103	—	102	—	—	—	—	—	—	—	—	—	1	19	—
	2	50	—	45	4	—	—	—	—	—	—	1	—	—	4	—
	3	24	—	24	—	—	—	—	—	—	—	—	—	—	1	—
	4	82	—	80	2	—	—	—	—	—	—	—	—	—	8	—
	5	90	—	86	2	—	—	—	—	—	—	1	1	—	12	—
	6	93	—	87	4	—	—	—	—	—	2	—	—	—	11	—
	7	46	—	44	2	—	—	—	—	—	—	—	—	—	5	—
		2914	—	2749	128	—	—	—	—	—	11	10	13	3	366	9

2 HENRY VI, Q. [First Part of the Contention of York and Lancaster.]

Act.	Scene.	Total Lines.	Prose.	Blank.	Heroic.	Short Rhyme.	Songs.	Alternates.	Sonnets.	Doggrel.	One Measure.	Two Measure.	Three Measure.	Four Measure.	Female Ending.	Extra Syllable.
I	1	171	—	160	6	—	—	—	—	—	1	3	—	1	14	—
	2	80	—	78	2	—	—	—	—	—	—	—	—	—	4	—
	3	167	—	162	—	—	—	—	—	—	—	1	2	2	6	—
	4	51	—	50	—	—	—	—	—	—	—	1	—	—	1	—
II	1	166	80	80	4	—	—	—	—	—	—	1	—	1	—	—
	2	70	22	48	—	—	—	—	—	—	—	—	—	—	—	—
	3	87	50	29	8	—	—	—	—	—	—	—	—	—	1	—
	4	82	—	82	—	—	—	—	—	—	—	—	—	—	2	—
III	1	190	—	176	8	—	—	—	—	—	—	—	1	5	10	—
	2	219	—	200	8	—	—	—	—	—	—	2	2	7	12	—
	3	23	—	17	—	—	—	—	—	—	—	—	6	—	1	—
IV	1	72	—	66	—	—	—	—	—	—	—	3	—	3	2	—
	2	158	158	—	—	—	—	—	—	—	—	—	—	—	—	—
	3	8	8	—	—	—	—	—	—	—	—	—	—	—	—	—
	4	27	—	25	2	—	—	—	—	—	—	—	—	—	—	—
	5	14	6	8	—	—	—	—	—	—	—	—	—	—	—	—
	6	15	15	—	—	—	—	—	—	—	—	—	—	—	—	—
	7	99	99	—	—	—	—	—	—	—	—	—	—	—	—	—
	8	35	—	34	—	—	—	—	—	—	—	—	1	—	—	—
	9	29	—	29	—	—	—	—	—	—	—	—	—	—	—	—
	10	44	19	25	—	—	—	—	—	—	—	—	—	—	—	—
V	1	130	—	113	6	—	—	—	—	—	—	4	3	4	1	—
	2	65	—	64	—	—	—	—	—	—	—	—	—	1	—	—
	3	30	—	28	2	—	—	—	—	—	—	—	—	—	—	—
		2032	457	1474	46	—	—	—	—	—	1	15	15	24	54	—

3 HENRY VI. Octavo. [True Tragedy of Richard Duke of York.]

Act.	Scene.	Total Lines.	Prose.	Blank.	Heroic.	Short Rhyme.	Songs.	Alternates.	Sonnets.	Doggrel.	One Measure.	Two Measure.	Three Measure.	Four Measure.	Female Ending.	Extra Syllable.
I	1	230	—	221	—	—	—	—	—	—	3	2	1	3	13	—
	2	54	—	52	—	—	—	—	—	—	1	1	—	—	5	—
	3	215	—	203	4	—	—	—	—	—	1	2	2	3	16	—
II	1	176	—	167	6	—	—	—	—	—	—	2	1	—	9	—
	2	168	—	154	6	—	—	—	—	—	1	2	3	2	7	—
	3	48	—	45	2	—	—	—	—	—	—	1	—	—	—	—
	4	12	—	11	—	—	—	—	—	—	—	1	—	—	2	—
	5	64	—	53	10	—	—	—	—	—	1	—	—	—	2	—
	6	102	—	97	2	—	—	—	—	—	2	—	1	—	9	—
III	1	43	—	41	—	—	—	—	—	—	—	1	1	—	4	—
	2	131	—	113	8	—	—	—	—	—	1	4	4	1	13	—
	3	168	—	155	8	—	—	—	—	—	1	2	2	—	10	—
IV	1	96	—	85	4	—	—	—	—	—	1	2	3	1	8	—
	2	22	—	21	—	—	—	—	—	—	—	—	1	—	5	—
	3	31	—	29	2	—	—	—	—	—	—	—	—	—	2	—
	5	24	—	20	2	—	—	—	—	—	—	—	1	1	—	—
	4	23	—	21	2	—	—	—	—	—	—	—	—	—	1	—
	7	57	—	55	—	—	—	—	—	—	—	—	2	—	2	—
	6	19	—	16	2	—	—	—	—	—	—	—	1	—	—	—
	8	29	—	27	—	—	—	—	—	—	—	—	1	1	1	—
V	1	78	—	70	—	—	—	—	—	—	—	—	—	2	9	—
	2	44	—	42	2	—	—	—	—	—	—	—	—	—	3	—
	3	20	—	17	2	—	—	—	—	—	1	—	—	—	—	—
	4	45	—	43	—	—	—	—	—	—	—	—	1	1	1	—
	5	74	—	68	—	—	—	—	—	—	1	1	3	1	7	—
	6	82	—	78	2	—	—	—	—	—	—	—	1	1	9	—
	7	46	—	46	—	—	—	—	—	—	—	—	—	—	4	—
		2101	—	1956	64	—	—	—	—	—	14	21	29	17	148	—

RICHARD III. [Begun by Peele and Marlow 1592, after the True Tragedy: recast and finished by Shakespeare as in Q 1594-5.]

Quarto version (abridged somewhat for stage reasons).

Act.	Scene.	Total Lines.	Prose.	Blank.	Heroic.	Short Rhyme.	Songs.	Alternates.	Sonnets.	Doggrel.	One Measure.	Two Measure	Three Measure.	Four Measure.	Female Ending.	Extra Syllable.
I	1	162	—	145	14	—	—	—	—	—	—	2	—	1	32	1
	2	252	—	232	2	—	—	—	—	—	1	1	16	—	43	1
	3	352	—	339	8	—	—	—	—	—	1	3	1	—	83	—
	4	284	63	209	6	—	—	—	—	—	1	2	3	—	36	—
II	1	140	—	135	2	—	—	—	—	—	1	1	1	—	11	2
	2	142	—	136	2	—	—	—	—	—	2	2	—	—	24	—
	3	46	—	39	2	—	—	—	—	—	1	1	1	2	5	1
	4	73	—	62	6	—	—	—	—	—	—	2	2	1	11	—
III	1	200	—	178	12	—	—	—	—	—	1	6	1	2	33	—
	2	125	—	117	—	—	—	—	—	—	—	3	3	2	23	—
	3	25	—	21	2	—	—	—	—	—	1	—	1	—	1	1
	4	109	—	102	2	—	—	—	—	—	1	2	1	1	19	—
	5	109	—	99	—	—	—	—	—	—	—	4	5	1	23	—
	6	14	—	12	2	—	—	—	—	—	—	—	—	—	7	—
	7	232	—	216	8	—	—	—	—	—	—	3	1	4	34	—
IV	1	91	—	83	2	—	—	—	—	—	—	2	1	3	23	—
	2	125	—	108	4	—	—	—	—	—	1	3	6	3	13	—
	3	57	—	49	4	—	—	—	—	—	1	1	2	—	15	—
	4	443	—	393	34	—	—	—	—	—	3	4	5	4	71	1
	5	20	—	18	—	—	—	—	—	—	1	—	—	1	4	—
V	1	29	—	27	2	—	—	—	—	—	—	—	—	—	5	—
	2	24	—	22	2	—	—	—	—	—	—	—	—	—	1	—
	3	348	—	308	22	—	—	—	—	—	2	5	6	5	62	4
	4	13	—	13	—	—	—	—	—	—	—	—	—	—	1	—
	5	41	—	36	4	—	—	—	—	—	—	—	1	—	3	—
		3456	63	3099	142	—	—	—	—	—	18	47	57	30	583	11

The prose in I 4 may be corrupted verse.

RICHARD III. Folio. [As far as V 3a this gives the acting version in use in 1622. It is not known who made it: but it contains many lines of the original omitted in the Quarto. From V 3b to the end it is supplemented from the 1602 Quarto. Probably the prompter's copy from which it was printed was deficient towards the conclusion.]

Act.	Scene.	Total Lines.	Prose.	Blank.	Heroic.	Short Rhyme.	Songs.	Alternates.	Sonnets.	Doggrel.	One Measure.	Two Measure.	Three Measure.	Four Measure.	Female Ending.	Extra Syllable.
I	1	162	—	145	14	—	—	—	—	—	—	2	—	1	31	1
	2	263	—	243	2	—	—	—	—	—	1	1	16	—	41	1
	3	355	—	342	8	—	—	—	—	—	—	4	1	—	75	—
	4	288	63	215	6	—	—	—	—	—	—	1	3	—	32	—
II	1	140	—	134	2	—	—	—	—	—	1	2	1	—	19	2
	2	153	—	146	2	—	—	—	—	—	2	3	—	—	29	—
	3	47	—	45	2	—	—	—	—	—	—	—	—	—	6	1
	4	73	—	65	6	—	—	—	—	—	—	1	1	—	13	—
III	1	200	—	178	12	—	—	—	—	—	1	6	—	3	39	—
	2	125	—	119	—	—	—	—	—	—	1	2	3	—	26	—
	3	25	—	23	2	—	—	—	—	—	—	—	—	—	2	1
	4	108	—	104	2	—	—	—	—	—	1	—	1	—	24	—
	5	109	—	104	—	—	—	—	—	—	—	2	1	2	27	—
	6	14	—	11	2	—	—	—	—	—	—	—	—	1	6	—
	7	245	—	232	12	—	—	—	—	—	—	1	—	—	37	—
IV	1	104	—	97	6	—	—	—	—	—	—	—	1	—	23	—
	2	106	—	93	4	—	—	—	—	—	2	2	5	—	17	—
	3	57	—	52	4	—	—	—	—	—	1	—	—	—	16	—
	4	540	—	501	36	—	—	—	—	—	—	1	1	1	98	1
	5	20	—	18	—	—	—	—	—	—	1	—	—	1	3	—
V	1	29	—	26	2	—	—	—	—	—	1	—	—	—	7	—
	2	24	—	22	2	—	—	—	—	—	—	—	—	—	1	—
	3	348	—	314	22	—	—	—	—	—	1	2	3	6	61	4
	4	13	—	13	—	—	—	—	—	—	—	—	—	—	2	—
	5	41	—	36	4	—	—	—	—	—	—	—	1	—	3	—
		3589	63	3278	152	—	—	—	—	—	13	30	38	15	638	11

TITUS ANDRONICUS. [Begun by Marlow and Peele 1592-3: finished by Peele 6th February, 1594, for Sussex' players: passed to the Chamberlain's men 1600.]

Act.	Scene.	Total Lines.	Prose.	Blank.	Heroic.	Short Rhyme.	Songs.	Alternates.	Sonnets.	Doggrel.	One Measure.	Two Measure.	Three Measure.	Four Measure.	Female Ending.	Extra Syllable.
I	1	495	—	467	24	—	—	—	—	—	2	—	1	1	17	1
II	1	135	—	126	6	—	—	—	—	—	—	2	1	—	3	1
	2	26	—	24	2	—	—	—	—	—	—	—	—	—	1	—
	3	306	—	293	10	—	—	—	—	—	—	1	1	1	34	—
	4	57	—	54	2	—	—	—	—	—	—	—	—	1	3	—
III	1	301	—	293	6	—	—	—	—	—	1	—	1	—	19	2
	2	85	—	77	6	—	—	—	—	—	—	1	1	—	8	1
IV	1	129	—	124	2	—	—	—	—	—	1	1	—	1	3	1
	2	180	—	167	4	—	—	—	—	—	1	3	4	1	27	2
	3	121	32	85	2	—	—	—	—	—	—	1	1	—	11	2
	4	113	11	88	8	—	—	4	—	—	—	—	1	1	8	1
V	1	165	—	149	12	—	—	—	—	—	—	1	2	1	31	1
	2	206	—	202	4	—	—	—	—	—	—	—	—	—	12	—
	3	204	—	169	34	—	—	—	—	—	—	1	—	—	23	—
		2523	43	2318	122	—	—	4	—	—	5	11	13	7	200	12

EDWARD III. [By a second hand and Shakespeare c. 1593.]

SHAKESPEARE'S PART.

Act.	Scene.	Total Lines.	Prose.	Blank.	Heroic.	Short Rhyme.	Songs.	Alternates.	Sonnets.	Doggrel.	One Measure.	Two Measure.	Three Measure.	Four Measure.	Female Ending.	Extra Syllable.
I	2b	77		32	45	—	—	—	—	—	—	—	—	—	2	—
II	1	458	—	407	42	—	—	—	—	—	1	5	2	1	48	—
	2	209	—	187	14	—	—	—	—	—	2	3	—	3	24	—
		744	—	626	101	—	—	—	—	—	3	8	2	4	74	—

THE SECOND HAND.

Act.	Scene.	Total Lines.	Prose.	Blank.	Heroic.	Short Rhyme.	Songs.	Alternates.	Sonnets.	Doggrel.	One Measure.	Two Measure.	Three Measure.	Four Measure.	Female Ending.	Extra Syllable.
I	1	169	—	152	16	—	—	—	—	—	—	1	—	—	3	—
	2a	89	—	83	6	—	—	—	—	—	—	—	—	—	10	—
III	1	191	—	178	10	—	—	—	—	—	—	1	2	—	2	—
	2	76	—	67	6	—	—	—	—	—	2	—	—	1	3	—
	3	227	—	219	8	—	—	—	—	—	—	—	—	—	3	—
	4	13	—	11	2	—	—	—	—	—	—		—	—	—	—
	5	114	—	110	2	—	—	—	—	—	—	1	1	—	1	—
IV	1	43	—	42	—	—	—	—	—	—	—	1	—	—	5	—
	2	85	—	81	4		—	—	—	—	—	—	—	—	4	—
	3	85	—	74	4	—	—	6	—	—	—	—	—	1	5	—
	4	160	—	154	4	—	—	—	—	—	1	—	1	—	14	—
	5	121	—	111	10	—	—	—	—	—	2	2	—	—	8	—
	6	62	—	57	4	—	—	—	—	—	—	—	1	—	8	—
	7	64	—	49	11	—	—	4	—	—	—	—	—	—	3	—
V	1	243	—	234	8		—	—	—	—	—	1	—	—	4	—
		1746	—	1622	95	—	—	10	—	—	5	7	5	2	73	—

IV.

THE LITERARY CAREER OF A SHAKESPEARE FORGER.*

IT is a curious illustration of the economical principle of supply and demand that whenever a literary commodity is much sought after on account of its excessive rareness the demand is met by a literary forgery. The history of Shakespeare criticism is diversified by upwards of half a dozen cases of this spurious supply, the first of which was in answer to the demand for Shakespeare manuscripts, and the last, extending over thirty years, was perpetrated with the object of satisfying the demand for Shakespeare history and textual emendation. As it is with the forger of the last century that we have now to deal, I will premise a few remarks on the subject of Shakespeare manuscripts. I am not sure it is generally known that we have no certain proof that a single line in Shakespeare's autograph was in existence at any time during the last century.† The fact is remarkable because it is not the

* Read at a Meeting of the Royal Society of Literature, March 27, 1878.

† We have but W. H. Ireland's report of the assertions of Mr. and Mrs. Williams, of Clopton House, in 1793, as to the destruction of 'a large basketful' of papers bearing the signature 'William Shakespeare'—*Authentic Account*, p. 5; *Confessions*, p. 31—a report which the late Mr. Wheler, of Stratford-on-Avon, who had the best opportunities of knowing the truth, assured Mr. J. O. Halliwell was utterly and entirely without foundation of fact.

case with any of Shakespeare's great rivals—*e.g.*, we have several letters and copies of verses written by Ben Jonson, and his autograph manuscript of *The Masque of Queens* is in the national repository. But of Shakespeare's writing we possess nothing more than half a dozen signatures, viz., the three to his will, the last being in the form 'by me, William Shakspere;' and those on the tags attached to the purchase deed of the tenth of March, 1612, and the mortgage deed of the eleventh of March, 1612: to which we may perhaps add the signature in the Museum copy of Florio's Montaigne; and we have also the rumour of another signature of Shakespeare, once on the tag of a fine in the Chapter House of Westminster (*Athenæum*, 1841, p. 428; 1843, p. 717). Whether the last signature is in existence is doubtful, for the very condition which leads to the mutilation of deeds for the sake of an autograph not unnaturally ends in its destruction. Its possessor may for a while enjoy the solitary satisfaction of having in his portfolio a treasure which every collector who knew of its existence would covet, but he will shrink from a disclosure which would brand his name with disgrace, and he will hardly allow the fragment to survive him.

It is incumbent on me now to give some account of the discovery and history of the two deeds to which Shakespeare's undoubted signature is attached; for it is to one of them that we are indebted for one of the Ireland forgeries. Besides the family of the Irelands, there are two persons unpleasantly mixed up with the fabrications: an attorney named Albany Wallis, and an actor named Montague Talbot. The critics have never seen their way to exonerate the former from complicity, nor the latter from active participation, in this discreditable hoax. Wallis was in partnership with one Troward, whose son will shortly be mentioned; and this firm were solicitors to the Rev. — Fetherstonhaugh, of Oxted, Surrey. In the year 1768 Wallis is said to have discovered among his client's title-deeds the mortgage deed of the eleventh of March, 1612, and, I suppose with his client's consent, Wallis presented it to Garrick. In 1790 Malone saw it in the possession of Garrick's widow, and he afterwards printed a transcript of it and a facsimile of the signature. In 1796, when the question of the orthography of the name Shakespeare was in discussion, Malone again applied to Mrs. Garrick for the production of the mortgage deed, in order to verify his facsimile; but the deed was gone. I have no doubt whatever that Wallis had surreptitiously gained possession of it, for it was soon used for a dishonest purpose by his friend W. H. Ireland. By a curious coincidence Wallis is said to have found at this very time the counterpart of the tenth of March, 1612, among Mr. Fetherstonhaugh's muniments. Malone inspected this also, and being satisfied of the genuineness of Shakespeare's signature appended to that deed published a facsimile of it.

It will be seen that at some time between 1790 and 1796 the mortgage deed had passed out of Mrs. Garrick's possession, and I have to add that this deed together with Wallis's presentation letter to Garrick is known to have found its way back into the office of Wallis and Troward. Now it is certain that about the year 1794 a fabricated deed, copied from the mortgage deed in question, and bearing spurious signatures of William

Shakespeare, Michael Fraser, and Elizabeth Fraser, was in the possession of Samuel Ireland.

The original mortgage deed was brought to the hammer in May, 1841, when it was knocked down to Mr. Elkins for £162. 15s.; and again in May, 1843 it was sold by auction to the Corporation of London for £145. It is now in the Guildhall Library.

The purchase deed was privately produced by young Troward in March, 1858, to Sir Frederick Madden, then the Keeper of the Manuscripts in the British Museum, and in the following June it was, on his recommendation, purchased by the trustees for £330. 15s. Large as this sum was, it was a better investment than that of the £130 which the trustees gave for the Florio signature on the recommendation of the Keeper of the Printed Books Department—a signature which is still doubted by the most competent palæographers, though it is certainly more ancient than the epoch of the Ireland forgeries. If there be still another specimen of Shakespeare's writing, it will be found in certain lines, undoubtedly in a sixteenth century handwriting, appended to a manuscript tragedy entitled *The History of Sir Thomas More*, in the Harleian Collection 7368. I trust it will not be long before this unique manuscript is reproduced in facsimile by one of the learned societies who give themselves to that kind of work.

But it is now time that we turn to the subject of the Ireland forgeries, premising that they constitute one of seven distinct sets of fabrications. Chief of the other half dozen are the nine (or more) fraudulent manuscripts purchased by Richard Fenton, barrister, in 1807, at a sale in Carmarthen. I have not learned in whose custody they are at present. As they are perhaps the best things of their kind that have ever been done, one regrets that the name of their perpetrator has never been discovered, though the place at which they were purchased seems to point at Montague Talbot, the actor.* There are other spurious matters closely associated with the names of William Chetwood, the stage-manager, Charles Macklin, the player and playwright, George Steevens, the editor, John Jordan, the ballad-monger, and some others. But by far the most important name in the roll of Shakespeare forgers, who flourished in the reign of George III, is William Henry Ireland. Despite all the Vindications, Authentic Accounts, Confessions, &c., that have been vouchsafed in the cause of truth, there still doth hang a cloud of mystery as well as of opprobrium over the family name. Mystery begins with the very name of the reputed forger: for though he never stooped so low as to adopt an *alias*, barring the 'M. H.' of the forgeries, it is still a question for settlement whether he had not another Christian name—indeed

* *A Tour in quest of Genealogy in Wales, Somerset, and Wilts, by a Barrister, with a number of Curious Fragments from a MS. Collection ascribed to Shakespeare.* 1811. We have an account of the purchase at p. 29, and of the contents at p. 187. The specimens are given on pp. 189, 190, 200, 202, 212, 233, 234, and 250. The spelling of these fragments is—*pace* Mr. Jeremiah's dictum—passable, if not unexceptionable. My own impression is, that they are from the same source as the Ireland forgeries. Montague Talbot, W. H. Ireland's confederate, once hailed from Carmarthen, where these fragments were bought. See *Vindication*, p. 12. Besides, the 24th manuscript in the schedule of unproduced papers—*Vindication*, p. 37—viz., 'Brief account of his [Shakespeare's] life in his own hand,' answers to No. 4 of the Fenton manuscripts.

Professor Dowden in his *Handbook* gives him only the Christian name of Samuel—and, after that point has been set at rest, whether our hero was the forger of the documents with which his name is associated, and with which he is credited in the *Bibliographer's Manual*. As if it were not enough that serious debate should be held whether Shakespeare was the author of Shakespeare: whether some other great man of that day (say Bacon alone, or Raleigh, or Bacon and Raleigh) did not produce the works of Shakespeare, just as a πάρεργον wrought during the brief spans which such overworked geniuses could steal from their professional leisure for the cultivation of the Muses—as if that were not enough, I say, a secondary discussion has been maintained whether a notorious forger, who on three occasions publicly confessed himself to be such, was not rather a great liar than a great forger: in a word, whether W. H. Ireland was the author of the Ireland Forgeries. Now it is to set at rest these questions of name and authorship that I have written this paper; and my excuse for once more calling attention to so well-worn a subject lies in the single fact that evidence has recently come to light, which enables me once for all to settle them.

Samuel Ireland, the Spitalfields weaver, like many another weaver, left weaving for literature, and opened a shop in Norfolk Street, Strand, for the sale of old books, prints, and other curiosities; and from selling books and prints took to making them. He had married the beautiful Anna Maria (? Irwin), and this union was blessed with four children: Samuel, William Henry, Anna Maria, and Jane: though as to No. 2 the blessing was at one time held in question, and poor Sam. senior, surviving Sam. junior, died in the full conviction that his second son had been little better than a curse. The elder-born son died early, and was thus, unknown to himself or his father, 'taken from the evil to come.' Thenceforth the younger son was, as I have learned from his nephew, familiarly called 'Sam.' His father calls him Sam. in the *Vindication*, pp. 14 and 15: Talbot calls him 'Sam.' in his declaration (*Vindication*, p. 52), in his letter (*Authentic Account*, p. 27), and in his Carmarthen letter (*Vindication*, p. 12), where Talbot writes of the forger both as 'Samuel' and 'Sam.' In fact from the death of the real Sam., the surviving son adopted the praenomen of Samuel, and signed himself 'S. W. H. Ireland.' Accordingly, on the title-page of his own copy of the *Returne from Pernassus* (4to, 1606), we find the initials, in his handwriting, 'S. W. H. I.:' to a declaration, an affidavit, an advertisement, and an undertaking, all printed by Samuel Ireland in his *Vindication*, 1796, at pp. 12, 29, 31, and 35, we find the signature 'S. W. H. Ireland;' and in the same book on p. 28 is an affidavit signed 'Samuel William Henry Ireland.' These papers, or at least some of them, are in the Manuscripts Department of the British Museum.* Moreover in the earliest fabricated deed, with the signature 'William

* In a copy of the *Authentic Account* in the British Museum is a manuscript note (unsigned) stating the report that W. H. Ireland was baptized at St. Clement Dane's, under the name of *William Henry Irwin*, and that his mother was a married woman separated from her husband. There is no such entry between 1772 and 1779 inclusive; and in 1794 or 5 W. H. I. was 18. The rumour is discredited by Mr. Arnold, *Fraser's Magazine*, August, 1860, p. 167.

Shakespeare,' the feigned recipient of Shakespeare's bounty is 'mye goode freynde Masterre William Henrye Irelande:' a fact which almost suggests that the forger, if 'Samuel,' was not 'William Henry'—for it would seem unlikely that he would insert his own exact Christian and surname in a fabrication, which he designed to pass off as genuine. Possibly it was this consideration which led Professor Dowden to conclude that the forger was christened simple 'Samuel.' Nevertheless it is certain that he was christened 'William Henry'—and nothing else.

The so-called 'Shakespeare Papers' which issued from the Ireland forge and—with two exceptions—viz., Nos. 15 and 16—were publicly exhibited in Norfolk Street—were—

1.—Shakespeare's Profession of Faith.

2.—Shakespeare's copy of his letter to Lord Southampton, and Lord Southampton's answer.

3.—Shakespeare's letter to Richard Cowley, with a pen-and-ink sketch of himself, &c.

4.—Shakespeare's letter to Anne Hathaway, with a lock of his hair.

5.—Stanzas to Ann Hathaway.

6.—Shakespeare's note of hand on John Hemynge, with J. H.'s receipt.

7.—Lease: Shakespeare to Michael Frazer and wife.

8.—Agreement between Shakespeare and Henry Condell.

9.—Agreement between Shakespeare and John Lowine.

10.—Two drawings of Shakespeare on one paper, &c., &c.

11.—Letter from Queen Elizabeth to Shakespeare: noted by himself.

12.—A manuscript of *King Lear.*

13.—Manuscript fragment of *Hamlet.*

14.—Several deeds witnessed by Shakespeare.*

15.—Several receipts, &c., on account of certain theatres.

16.—Several letters signed by Shakespeare, &c.

17.—*Vortigern.* A manuscript tragedy in W. H. Ireland's simulated handwriting.

18.—*Henry II.* A manuscript tragedy in W. H. Ireland's ordinary handwriting (three pp. only having been written in the simulated hand).†

Palæography must have been unknown in those days, or the handwriting alone would, at the first glance, have betrayed the imposture. Nay, further, archaic spelling must have been a wholly neglected subject, or the spelling of these papers would have covered them with ridicule. Both these remarks apply with equal force to Ireland and Chatterton: for there never was a period when the writing or the spelling adopted by either had been in use. Both of them appear to have known but little beyond the indefinite fact, that in earlier times it was the custom in many cases to write y for i, to double the consonants, and to append an e. Ireland works this rule in so mechanical a fashion that it is difficult to understand how such men as Warton, Parr, Heard, Valpy, &c., refrained from laughter when they first examined the papers: *e.g.*,

* We do not know who has the three deeds mentioned in the *Vindication*, p. 25.

† Yet the British Museum has a manuscript copy entirely in the simulated hand.

Thatte thou haste perrepennedycularelye felle:

in *Lear*, and the inscription on the manuscript play, signed 'Wm. Shakespeare,' who is made to write that his play

> Ifse fromme Masterre Hollinneshedde I have
> inne somme lyttle deparretedde fromme
> hymme butte thatte Libbertye will notte
> I truste be blamedde bye mye gentle
> Readerres.

It is scarcely credible that Ireland himself should not have known that he was here putting the skeleton-key to the fraud into the hands of the archæologist.

Passing over the miserable rubbish which fills the letter and verses to 'Anna Hatherrewaye,' in the letter to Southampton, where the playwright is made to tell the Peer, that gratitude 'is a Budde which Blloffommes Blooms butte never dyes' (how exquisite must have been Ireland's delight in these reduplicated ll which no scribe ever doubled before!), the Profession of Faith,* where Shakespeare is made to liken the Almighty to a 'sweete Chickenne'—of all living creatures—and the amazing address to the forger's feigned namesake, where it is said that 'Shakespeares Soule restelefle inne the Grave shalle uppe Agayne ande meete hys freynde hys Ireland'—where one would naturally expect to hear of his meeting his God (all which makes us wonder how any educated man in his senses could have received these papers as genuine), we may note that some of

* Suggested to W. H. I. by the Profession of Faith of John Shakespeare, which was fabricated by Jordan, but taken for genuine by Ireland.—See *Confessions*, p. 56.

them, like some of the Fenton papers, carry their spuriousness unmistakably on their face. Just as in one of the latter we have Shakespeare telling how he had sat for his portrait to Succaro (*i. e.*. Zucchero, see *Tour*, p. 201)[1] and another bears date before Shakespeare was born; so in the endorsement of Queen Elizabeth's letter to Shakespeare his theatre is called 'the Globe bye Thames;' and in the lease to Fraser and wife, the houses leased are described as 'abutting close to the Globe theatre by Black Fryers London.' Yet we have it on unimpeachable evidence that when Warton and Parr had read all the papers including the Profession of Faith, the former thus addressed the elder Ireland: 'Mr. Ireland, we have very fine things in our church service, and our litany abounds with beauties, but here is a man [who] has distanced us all;' and that 'Boswell fell upon his knees, and, in a tone of enthusiasm and exultation, thanked God that he had lived to witness this discovery, and exclaimed that he could now die in peace.' Whether Parr did, as the Irelands assert, agree to Warton's apostrophe, or not, it is certain that the first certificate of authenticity was actually drawn up by Parr, who had expressed dissatisfaction with that drafted by Boswell as 'too feebly expressed.'—(*Vindication*, p. 20.)

The forgeries, by whomsoever executed, were written during the years 1794 and part of 1795; and in the early part of the latter year all the papers, with the exception of *Vortigern* and *Henry II*, were on view at Samuel Ireland's house in Norfolk

[1] Cosway's portrait of Shakespeare was attributed to Zucchero—or François—spurious beyond doubt.

Street. The tragedy of *Vortigern*, or as it was then called, *Vortigern and Rowena*, was performed at Drury Lane Theatre on April 2, 1796. At a preconcerted signal the play was interrupted towards the end of Vortigern's soliloquy in the second scene of the third act: the words are addressed to Death, and the four concluding lines are—

> And when this solemn mockery is o'er,
> With icy hand thou tak'st him by the feet,
> And upward so, till thou dost reach the heart,
> And wrap him in the cloak of lasting night.

Of course there is here a glance at Mrs. Quickly's account of Falstaff's death, and the last line is a close imitation of Shakespeare's language.

As usual the testimony of eye and ear witnesses is not consistent; but it is not difficult to elicit the fact from their discrepant statements. I will cite but two witnesses. A correspondent to *Notes and Queries* writes (2nd S., iii, 442):

> At last John Kemble . . . brought the question to its climax; for in a passage which (as I best recollect) described the progress of death upon the human frame, he exclaimed 'then catch him by the throat,' and grasping his own throat with a rather ludicrous action, and pausing, a slight laugh arose, and he himself appeared to be struggling with convulsive laughter, and then burst out a roar of genuine mirth from the pit, which was taken up by the whole house.

That Kemble, in the line 'With icy hand thou tak'st him by the feet,' should have substituted 'throat' for 'feet,' is incredible; for Ireland who charges Kemble with betraying the piece does not charge him with altering a word in it, but with having 'reiterated the line ["And when this solemn mockery is o'er"] with an expression the most pointedly sarcastic and acrimonious it is possible to conceive:' and if Kemble did not substitute 'throat' for 'feet,' it is not at all likely that he would have seized his own throat (unless it was to choke a laugh): besides 'An Octogenarian,' writing in *Notes and Queries*, 2nd S., iii, 492, corroborates Ireland's account in every particular.

Four publications on the authenticity of the Papers had preceded the representation of *Vortigern*. Malone's *Inquiry*, demolishing the whole imposture, was published the day after the *fiasco*, and was the signal for further publications attacking, defending, or vindicating the forgeries. Five volumes, viz., those of Woodward (by some the 'Familiar Verses' were attributed to one Orton), White, Sir Bate and Lady Dudley, and Hargrave, as well as the renowned 'Precious Relics,' are humorous or abusive, mostly in the nature of parodies: while those of Boaden, Colonel Webb, Waldron, Wyatt, Malone, Caulfield, Chalmers, Cobbett, Oulton, Harding, and Matthias, and two anonymous works, are serious discussions of the authenticity—a question which would seem unworthy of such treatment, and a proper subject for ridicule. The historical question was reopened by myself in 1859, and provoked two admirable replies, the one by the late Mr. T. J. Arnold, F.S.A. and police magistrate, which was published in *Fraser's Magazine* for August, 1860, the other in the *London Review* for October, 1860, not improbably from the pen of the editor, Dr. Charles Mackay. These two together furnish an excellent and accurate history of the Ireland Forgeries, leaving nothing more to be said, but what relates to sources of information not accessible to the public at the time those accounts were written. The earlier critiques range over the period 1796—1800, both inclusive. The few writers who had believed in and defended the papers had given in by 1797; and Fortune, having 'spurned down her late beloved'—whether we refer to the elder Sam. or the younger man so nicknamed—not one votary remained who was willing to accompany 'his declining foot.' Both father and son were covered with abuse, and neither was ever forgiven by his contemporaries for a practice which, whether innocent or not, had done the excellent work of unmasking the impostors of criticism. I have said 'not one:' but there was one, if not two. Gore Langton, who had refused to inspect the papers (as Steevens and Malone had done), evinced the kindliest disposition towards the elder Ireland: and William Cobbett took occasion to pat the younger Ireland on the back and denounce the fresh-growing idolatry of 'the immortal bard,' whom he considered as a fit subject for blame as well as praise, and utterly unfit to stand as England's typical poet.

I will say no more of these eighteenth century writers. For fifty years the subject slumbered; but it cropped up again on the publication of Mr. J. P. Collier's *Notes and Emendations*, which heralded the advent of an entirely new 'Shakespeare Controversy,' and the detection of a series of fabrications far more skilful and injurious than those which had astonished the contemporaries of Johnson. My unfortunate note on the Ireland Forgeries, published in 1859, was called forth by an anonymous one printed in *Willis's Current Notes* for December, 1855, and subsequently owned by a literary gentleman who was once an assistant to William Hone, and who had married his daughter. We may, accordingly, date the rise of the second series of publications on the Ireland Forgeries, in that month. By that time W. H. Ireland had been dead about twenty years. He was, in fact, born in or about 1776,* and died in 1835 in his 60th year.

Up to 1853 it was generally accepted, that W. H. Ireland was the sole and unassisted forger (unless his friend Talbot had given him some small help), and Samuel Ireland the dupe of his son. It seemed, however, that there was one dissentient, who had held his peace for twenty years after his witness had died, and who then gave the world, at second-hand, that witness's testimony. Mr. Burn, the editor of the serial in question, wrote as follows—NEMO being the signature of a previous correspondent in the columns of *Willis's Current Notes*:

NEMO is in error in supposing him [W. H. Ireland] to have been 'the author of the Shakespeare Forgeries.' His father, Samuel Ireland was the original deviser of the whole affair. He had succeeded so well in befooling 'professed judges' of the original designs by Hogarth; that, prompted by his needy circumstances, he let fly at a higher game, and befouled the shrine of England's dramatic bard! It was Samuel Ireland's eldest daughter who wrote the imitations of the dramatist; the younger one assisted, and the redoubtable William Henry was merely a copier. It was Samuel Ireland who began by collecting books of Shakespeare's time, fabricated manuscript notes and inserted them in the books as if written

* In his *Confessions*, p. 312, he says he was 'scarcely seventeen years and a-half old' when he wrote the forgeries. If this means, in 1794, he would have been born in 1776 or 1777.

by the immortal bard, when finding them greatly admired, he persisted till their frequency might have divulged the nefariousness of the transaction, to all but those who were stupidly blind. In one of his freaks, Samuel Ireland desirous of accommodating the world with a portrait of the irritable Shakespearian Critic John Dennis, and not aware there was really one extant, engraved by Vandergucht—ventured on one copied from an *original* drawing by Hogarth, in the second volume of his Graphic Illustrations of that celebrated painter. It is almost nugatory to observe Hogarth never troubled himself about John Dennis of theatrical thunder notoriety, and the portrait there presented is a fiction by Samuel Ireland, though received as genuine by many Hogarthian Collectors. Should NEMO's desire be still unsatiated, the writer, to whom William Henry Ireland was long personally known, may possibly communicate some particulars hitherto but very imperfectly known. Let this be generally understood, the 'Confessions' published by him were a tissue of lies from beginning to end, and the original idea of the volume was caused by an irresistible impulse at the moment, that of raising the wind, as he himself assured the writer—

When needs must, the Devil drives!*

Willis's Current Notes, December, 1855.

I know not whether NEMO ever asked for more: I know I did, both by letter to *Willis's Current Notes*, and by private letter to the editor: but Mr. Burn would not break silence. I then sent a statement of the facts to *Notes and Queries*, but Mr. Thoms would not insert it. Finally I sent a note on the subject to Mr. Hotten, for his *Adversaria*, which appeared in the No. for May 2nd, 1857. On the 2nd also appeared in *Notes and Queries* (2nd S., iii, 344), an article from the pen of Mr. William Bates, of Birmingham, whose opinion I shall presently cite.

My note in Hotten's *Adversaria* treated Mr. Burn's com-

* An error for 'Needs must, when the Devil drives.'

munication as a hoax. That was more than he could stand, and he indignantly came up to the scratch; but the facts he was thus made to impart had little or no reference to the question of W. H. Ireland's authorship of the Shakespeare forgeries: they concerned his private life, and as I have no wish to 'draw his frailties from their dread abode,' I shall not repeat Mr. Burn's statements. I will only say that he insisted upon it that 'W. H. Ireland was one of the greatest liars that ever lived;' and he seemed to think that the establishment of this proposition removed all doubts as to the truth of Ireland's private confession to himself. The logic is not so bad as it looks, for a man may lie for a purpose to the public, yet speak truth to his friend. It is always difficult to determine what degree of credence should be given to the assertion of an untrustworthy man, and the difficulty is not diminished in a case where the witness has committed himself to two contradictory statements. In the case of the Simonides forgeries, which received full discussion at a meeting of this Society, a similar difficulty ultimately arose; for after the detection of the forgery of the Uranius manuscript the arch-forger, while maintaining the genuineness of that palimpsest, publicly declared that he had fabricated the Codex Sinaiticus. But in the case of the Ireland manuscripts there is just a doubt whether Mr. Burn has not misrepresented or coloured Ireland's private confession. My own conviction is that very little weight can be attached to the accuracy of Mr. Burn's report. In 1859 I thought differently, and committed myself to a note on the Ireland forgeries, appended to my first Shakespeare book, which I now deeply regret.

Mr. Bates relied upon three points—I. Ireland's advertisement in the London papers asserting the innocence of his father (*Vindication*, p. 30). II. His solemn declaration that he was the author and writer of the forgeries (*Authentic Account*, p. 42). III. His reiteration of both assertions three years before his death (*Vortigern*, 2nd edition, p. vii).

But if, as Mr. Barn says, Ireland was the greatest liar that ever lived, these allegations go for nothing: but not knowing with what object Ireland was induced to make a private confession to Mr. Barn, and being far from sure that in those needy days he did not make it with a view to literary employment, I should not be disposed to attach more weight to his confidential than to his public avowal. But whatever we are to think of Mr. Barn's communication, I am happily in a position to clear the name of Samuel Ireland from the foul aspersions which have been cast upon it.

In the first place it is as well to remember what was the elder Ireland's dying declaration. I am not disposed as a matter of course to accept unchallenged the last dying speech and confession of any man, but I give Mr. Ireland's for what it may be worth. Dr. Latham, who attended him in his last illness, in 1800, records it at p. 176 of his once-valued work on Diabetes, published in 1810:—he writes 'notwithstanding the world did not give Mr. Ireland credit for his assertions respecting his concurrence [with] or even connivance at his son's literary fraud, yet in justice to his memory I think myself here called upon, since I have this opportunity, to record it as his death-bed declaration that he was totally ignorant of the deceit, and was equally a believer in the authenticity of the manuscripts as *(sic)* those who were the most credulous.'

Mr. Arnold, in the article already mentioned, like Mr. Bates, lays stress upon W. H. Ireland's three statements, and believes in the honesty of his confession and his exoneration of his father, adding that even if the *Confessions* be not trustworthy throughout there 'is no ground for implicating his father or any other member of his family;' nevertheless this writer continues thus: 'What cannot fail to induce some feeling of doubt in the truth of W. H. Ireland's narrative is the fact that a comparatively uneducated youth should without co-operation have produced, not only such a mass of manuscripts in so short a time, but that he should have been able to fabricate a drama of nearly 3,000 lines which, by any sane person, could be received as the poetry of Shakespeare.' But, he adds, 'there is no evidence to counterbalance William Henry's positive and repeated assurance that he received no assistance from any quarter. If there were any one towards whom suspicion might be directed, it would be to Mr. Montague Talbot, the intimate friend and confidant of young Ireland, and to some extent his aider and abettor in the fraud. Talbot, to adopt W. H. Ireland's phrase, was "a friend of the muses:" he undoubtedly offered to assist in the fabrication of *Vortigern*.' (See *Confessions*, pp. 126—131.) Mr. Arnold's conclusion is that in any event the elder Ireland must be acquitted of all share in the forgeries either as author or abettor; in fact, that he was simply the dupe of his son. Moreover, Mr. Burn's assertion is discredited by the counter-assertion of another friend of W. H. Ireland, who informed

Mr. Arnold that William Henry 'was very communicative as to his Shakespearian fabrications—[that] he never said in plain terms that his father was privy to his imposture, but somewhat suspiciously hinted doubts as to his total ignorance of what was so mysteriously going on.'

On the other hand the writer in the *London Review* seems willing to admit that the elder Ireland is not free from the suspicion at least of connivance. He writes 'It is not easy to believe that Samuel Ireland was wholly innocent of complicity in the fraud of which he was the willing agent. But there is no inculpatory evidence, and there are some circumstances which tend to exonerate him altogether. Perhaps the strongest ground of suspicion against him is that he did not betray any suspicion himself. * * * * Three years after the publication of his son's confessions he declared in his preface to *Vortigern*, that not even that disclosure, nor all the arguments of the critics founded upon internal evidence, could induce him to believe that great part of the papers were fabricated by any individual or set of men of that day.' I do not see that the latter assertion favours the suspicion against him: on the contrary, it appears to me that, if he himself were the author or the concoctor of the forgeries, he would not have shewn the least anxiety to relieve his contemporaries from the odium of the fraud. But if he were conscious of his own innocence he might well feel that an excuse might be found, not only for his own credulity, but for that of such men as Parr and Warton, by attributing to some of the papers a value and an antiquity which they did not possess.

In fact, in view of all the circumstances, the writer in the *London Review* 'acquits Mr. Ireland, senior, of any guilty participation in the transaction. * * * * On many occasions we have heard W. H. Ireland vindicate his father from all complicity in the forgeries, direct or indirect, with an earnestness and warmth that at all events looked like truth, and we know that Mr. Talbot believed Mr. Samuel Ireland to have been the dupe of his son':—and this was the opinion of Dr. Drake, recorded in his *Shakespeare and his Times.*

I said that the excuse for this paper was the fact that evidence had recently come to light settling, or at least materially tending to settle, the question of authorship. Last summer the Trustees of the British Museum, through the agency of Mr. Robson, of Cranbourn Street, purchased of Samuel Ireland's nephew the whole of his Literary Remains. My own examination of these voluminous papers has removed from my mind all doubt as to the complete exculpation of the old man. The Remains consist of three thick quarto volumes besides a mass of miscellanea. These volumes are (1) a Scrap-Book of newspaper-cuttings, bills, caricatures, &c., relating to the forgeries, with manuscript notes by the collector: (2) his Correspondence with Sheridan, Linley, Wallis, Kemble, Talbot, &c.: and (3) Samuel Ireland's carefully kept diary, with letters from his son, and the feigned Mr. H.*

There are also the agreement between father and son as to the delivery of the papers, the declarations of faith in the authenticity of the papers, with the autograph signatures of

* On p. 146, 'M. H.' should be 'Mr. H.'

the dupes, four deeds with forged signatures, and several forgeries not included in the 'Miscellaneous Papers.'

Poor old Sam. never emerged from the cloud of obloquy which covered him as soon as the Shakespeare-bubble had burst. His favourite and last-surviving son forsook him, to seek his bread in a precarious way by literary hack-work. The old man never looked up again. He probably *thought* with Othello, though he did not actually speak it.

> It *is* too true an evil:—
> And what's to come of my despised time
> Is nought but bitterness.

He survived his humiliation and disgrace but four years. Among the Remains lately acquired by the British Museum are two portraits of Samuel Ireland, the one being a caricature, printed, as was the custom of the day, in a pink or pale red ink.

Of W. H. Ireland there is but one engraved portrait; a copy is in the British Museum, and I inserted another in the Moncreiff-Mackay quarto volume of Specimens of W. H. Ireland's Forgeries, which I presented last spring to the Birmingham Shakespeare Memorial Library.* The only miniature of him was painted on ivory by Samuel Drummond, A.R.A., and this represents a man past middle life, having the appearance of a handsome beau, not a little made up. This was hung by myself, last May, in the Library of Shakespeare's Birthplace; and it is the property of the trustees.

* This was destroyed in the disastrous fire of January 11th, 1879.

W. H. Ireland married one of the Culpeppers of Kent Castle (a family famous in the Civil Wars), the widow of Captain Paget, R.N., nephew to the Marquis of Anglesea. It is said that the marriage was not a happy one. He appears at all times to have been able to earn a competency. Once he was brought under the notice of Royalty, and was engaged to write a sort of masque for the Princess Elizabeth. Besides writing two pieces for the occasion of the Frogmore Fête, he was engaged for four days in the preparations for it: and his exertions were rewarded by the offer of a £5 note. I am glad to say he had the manliness to refuse it. He died May 2, 1835. His literary career is represented by over twenty publications—printed books and pamphlets—not a few of which are now lying upon the table.

Supplementary Note.

W. H. Ireland's literary career, as evidenced by his printed writings and manuscript remains, was scarcely worthy of his remarkable talents. The Shakespeare epoch, during which the *Authentic Account*, *Vortigern*, *Henry II*, and the *Shakespearian Hunt* (a series of papers contributed to the *Oracle*, a periodical edited by James Boaden), were produced and published, closed at the end of the last century. Then followed a period during which he wrote fiction and poetry; the former being represented by three novels, and the latter by a drama, and a volume of *Rhapsodies*: and he now rewrote his account of the Shakespeare forgeries, and published it, with a mass of gossip, in a volume entitled *Confessions*, &c. This book, which is, I fear, more amusing than trustworthy, was reprinted in facsimile by Mr. J. Pearson in 1872 (*circa*); a fact which proves that the first edition had become very scarce, and that there was still a demand for it.

In 1807 Ireland made a fresh start, and printed his first satirical piece, *The Modern Ship of Fools*, an imitative poem called *Neglected Genius* in 1812: his cleverest book, if indeed it were his, *Chalcographimania* in 1814: and *Scribbleomania* in 1815. In the *Chalcographimania* he is said to have had material aid from Caulfield the printseller and T. Coram: but Ireland's cloven foot once more displays itself in the frontispiece, which is a pretended portrait of the famous Jester 'Wil. Somers.'

In 1822 he came out in a new character, viz., as historian of France and translator from the French. First appeared his account of the Bourbons, called *France for Seven Years*, and soon after his English version of Voltaire's infamous *La Pucelle*. In 1823 he translated Philarète Chasles's *coup d'essai*, entitled *Mémoires d'une Jeune Grecque*. In 1824 appeared his *Memoires of Jeanne d'Arc*: and he now contributed to the continuation of Granger's *Biographical History of England*. In 1828 he published a *Life of Napoleon*, and *The Last Will and Testament of Napoleon Bonaparte*.

There is also a *New History of the County of Kent* by W. H. Ireland, in 4 vols., 1828. I do not know whether the author was the Shakespeare forger.

The concluding epoch of Ireland's life began in 1830, with a fresh series of political squibs: *The Political Devil, Reform, Britannia's Cat o' Nine Tails,* and *Constitutional Parodies.* Copies of these exceedingly scarce tracts, together with seven of those already mentioned, were sold for me by Messrs. Sotheby, Wilkinson, and Hodge (I should say *given away*) on April 7, 1879.

Of Ireland's manuscript remains I know of only the following six:

The Original Fabrications. In the British Museum. Bohn's Lowndes, 2322.

A Full and Explanatory Account of the Shakespearian Forger, by myself the writer, William Henry Ireland. Folio. Bohn's Lowndes, 2323.

The Life of the Old, Old, very Old Man Thomas Parr. By W. H. Ireland. Illustrated by drawings, engraved portraits, &c. Formerly in the Marquis of Donigall's collection. Large folio.

Stanzas to Miss Clara Fisher, by W. H. Ireland. Illustrated by engraved portraits. Quarto.

Monody on Shakespeare. Quarto.

Frogmore Fête, as written by me, W. H. Ireland, in 1802, at the Request of the Princess Elizabeth. Illustrated with portrait of the Princess Elizabeth. 28pp. Quarto. The last three bound in one volume were sold for me by Messrs. Sotheby, Wilkinson, and Hodge for the contemptible sum of 8s.

Signatures of Departed English and Foreign Potentates and Eminent Characters; or Death's Dance among the Reliques of the Departed. Illuminated from Holbein. This, which contains 144 imitated signatures, is still in my library, having been bought in for £1. 11s.

I may be allowed to note, in conclusion, that my library also possesses a special copy of the *Authentic Account,* 1796, which has twenty eight insertions; as follows:

1.—Three fabricated signatures of Shakespeare.
2.—Fabricated signature of Shakespeare to the Deed of Fraser.
3.— ,, ,, Michael Fraser.
4.—Sketch of the quintin seal affixed to same.

5.—Genuine impressions of the jug-water-mark.
6.—Sketch of the jug-water-mark.
7.—Shakespeare's Profession of Faith.
8.—Fac-simile of Lord Southampton's signature.
9.—Fabricated signature of Lord Southampton.
10.— „ Letter from Shakespeare to Richard Cowley.
11.— „ promissory note, Shakespeare to Heminge.
12.— „ signature of Heminge.
13.—Fac-simile of Heminge's signature.
14.—Love-letter of Shakespeare to Anne Hathaway.
15.—Fabricated signature of Queen Elizabeth.
16.—Fac-simile of Queen Elizabeth's signature.
17.—Note to Queen Elizabeth's spurious epistle in Shakespeare's fabricated hand.
18.—Fabricated manuscript passage in *King Lear*.
19.— „ signature of Lowin.
20.— „ „ Shakespeare to the Deed of Lowin.
21.— „ receipt for cash for playing before Lord Leicester, signed Wm. Shakespeare.
22.—Fac-simile of Lord Leicester's signature.
23.—Manuscript of passage in *Vortigern*.
24.—Fabricated signature of Shakespeare to the Deed with Condell.
25.— „ „ Condell.
26.—Armorial bearings of the Ireland Family.
27.—Verses in the handwriting of Anna Maria Ireland.
28.—Original portrait of Anna Maria Ireland as a girl.

It was not to the credit of the trade, that the members who attended the sale allowed this copy to be bought in for £2. 5s., a sum which very inadequately represents its value.

Another copy 'corrected throughout by the author for a new edition' was sold for me by Messrs. Sotheby, Wilkinson, and Hodge, April 7, 1879, and fetched £1. 7s. It had W. H. Ireland's autograph letter to the publisher, Debrett, prefixed: and on the title the autograph signatures of Debrett and J. P. Kemble. On the back of title Kemble writes that Allen's copy sold for £1.

The fragments of a play, entitled *The Virgin Queen*, printed by Waldron in 1796, must not be confounded with any of the 'Shakespeare Papers' fabricated by Ireland. In the 'Deed of Trust to John Hemynge' mention is made of an 'Interlude called ye Virgin Queene.' No such a piece was among the papers, though doubtless Ireland intended to fabricate it, had the bubble not burst so soon. As it is, the fragments so called were probably written by George Steevens, or by Waldron himself, to shew how easy it was to write like Shakespeare (!) if only, as Thomas Hood said, *one has the mind.*

V.

THE ELEGY ON BURBADGE.

RICHARD Burbadge, the famed tragedian of the King's Company, the original actor in all their chief tragic characters, survived Shakespeare nearly two years. He is said to have 'dyed on Saturday in Lent the 13th of March 1618.'* 'A Funerall Ellegye' on his death (having eighty-two, eighty-six, or one hundred and twenty-four lines, according to the particular version) has been handed down to our times in no less than seven manuscripts and six printed versions. Let me first speak of the latter. It was first printed by Joseph Haslewood, in the *Gentleman's Magazine*, June 1825, vol. xcv, part i, p. 498: secondly, about half of it was given in a foot-note to Mr. J. P. Collier's *History of Dramatic Poetry and Annals of the Stage*, 1831, vol. i, pp. 430-2: thirdly, about as much of it (from a different version) in his *New Particulars regarding the Works of Shakespeare*, 1836, pp. 29-31: where, in a foot-note to p. 27, he mentions having seen two other manuscript copies, one alluding to *A King and No King*: and, fourthly, the whole (in a still different version) in his *Memoirs of the Principal Actors in the Plays of Shakespeare*, printed for the 'Shakespeare Society,'

* From a folio volume in the library of Mr. Alfred Huth.

vol. xxvii, 1846, p. 52. Since that time the Elegy was not again reprinted till it appeared in the magnificent Catalogue of Mr. Huth's library, prepared by Mr. F. S. Ellis, where it is printed (in two versions) from the only two manuscripts in that collection. Besides these two, there are, I am told, four other perfect manuscripts of the Elegy: one at Warwick Castle, and three in Sir Thomas Phillipps's library at Cheltenham. There is also an imperfect draft of it in the Record Office (MSS. Jac. I. No. fol. 28: S.P. D. 1619, p. 26).

In the first edition of *Shakespeare's Centurie of Prayse*, 1874, p. 89, under date 1620, I quoted the following nine lines from the Elegy as printed by Haslewood, under the impression that, despite the two concluding couplets, they did allude to a representation of *Hamlet* in the funeral scene of the fifth act.

> Hee's gon and with him what a world are dead.
> Oft have I seen him leape into a grave
> Suiting ye person (wc^h^ hee us'd to have)
> Of a mad lover, wth so true an eye,
> That there I would have sworne hee meant to dye.
> Oft have I seene him play this part in jest
> So lively, y^t^ spectators, and the rest
> Of his crewes, whilst hee did but seeme to bleed,
> Amazed, thought hee had bene deade indeed.

In a version of the Elegy, which is in a folio volume in Mr. Huth's collection, these lines appear with the interpolation of four others after the first line of that extract: thus—

> hee's gone & wth him what A world are dead.
> which he reviv'd, to be revived soe,
> no more young Hamlett, ould Heironymoe

kind Leer, the Greved Moore, and more beside,
that lived in him; have now for ever dy'de,
oft have I seene him, leap into the Grave
sm[?]iting the person, wch he seem'd to have
of A sadd Lover, with soe true an Eye
that theer I would have sworne, he meant to dye.

It seemed to me then (*i. e.*, in 1873-4) and it seems to me now that these four lines were a purposed interpolation, intended, by the association of two plays so much alike in plot as *Hamlet* and *The Spanish Tragedy*, to fix the allusion to one of them at least, and to drag in the names of other tragic heroes in Shakespeare. But I did not at that time study the Elegy with sufficient care to perceive that not only certain passages in it, which appear as additions to the version in Mr. Huth's octavo volume, but the entire elegy, despite the pretence of early seventeenth century spelling, belongs to a period long subsequent to Burbadge's death. In the second edition of *Shakespeare's Centurie of Prayse*, 1879, p. 131, some extracts are given by the editor, Miss L. Toulmin-Smith, under the conjectural date 1618-19, from both of Mr. Huth's manuscript versions: she having taken it for granted that the Elegy in its entirety was the antique it pretended to be. While this portion of the *Centurie* was at press, a controversy was being carried on in the *Academy* (January, 1879) as to the correctness of Mr. Irving's impersonation of Hamlet at Ophelia's grave. The prince, as personated by him, does not leap into Ophelia's grave; and it was questioned whether Shakespeare intended Hamlet and Laertes to grapple with each other standing in the grave, or outside. The sanction for the once-prevalent practice of placing the struggle in the grave lies in the concurrence of all the early editions of the play in the stage direction 'Laertes leapes into the grave,' without any direction for his getting out again; and in the fact that the Quarto of 1603 has the conformable stage direction 'Hamlet leapes in after Laertes;' which is, however, not found in any other old copy.

Mr. F. J. Furnivall having, in the course of the discussion, called Mr. Moy Thomas's attention to the evidence which the Elegy, if genuine, would afford, the latter gentleman replied in the same periodical of January 18th and 25th, 1879. From his letters I make the following large extracts:

There are allusions in the poem which are not to be reconciled with the assumption that Hamlet is the lover referred to. A more serious difficulty, however, arises from the doubtful authenticity of the poem published for the first time more than two centuries after the period at which, if genuine, it must have been written. As Mr. Furnivall observes, "the after [introductory?] lines naming Hamlet, &c., printed by Mr. Collier, are evidently forged;" but if so the whole poem must come under suspicion. The occasions on which Mr. Collier has had the misfortune to be the instrument of giving to the world, as authentic, documents of an unquestionably fictitious character have, I admit, been so many and so grave that no pretended ancient manuscript can have a claim to be treated as genuine on the mere ground of respect due to his judgment and lifelong devotion to the study of old English literature. But it is just to Mr. Collier to observe that the distinction which Mr. Furnivall on this occasion draws between that gentleman and Mr. Haslewood is not supported by the facts of the case. It was, no doubt, Mr. Collier who first published the "elegy" on Burbage in its more complete form; but in so doing (*History of English Dramatic Poetry, &c.*, vol. i., p. 430), he distinctly named Mr. Haslewood as his authority. His words are:—

"In the *Gentleman's Magazine* for June 1825, Mr. Haslewood printed an elegy on the death of R. Burbage long preserved in MS., and he subsequently met with another copy of the same production (for which I have to thank him), with the important addition of some lines naming four of the parts in which Burbage especially excelled—viz., Hamlet, Hieronimo, Lear, and probably Othello."

Mr. Haslewood was, I believe, at that time (1831) and for a year or two afterwards living at his house in Addison Road, Kensington; and it seems impossible—deeply interested as he was in studies of this kind—that he could have failed to see Mr. Collier's work, or to become aware that he had thus been made directly responsible for the fuller version of the poem which, on the principle of *falsum in uno*, must, I fear, now be placed in the long and melancholy catalogue of spurious documents which perplex the student of Elizabethan dramatic literature and history. It is, I think, more to the purpose to observe that though the stage direction "Hamlet leapes in after Laertes" is found in the grossly defective and certainly unauthorised Quarto of 1603, it is not to be found either in the complete play as published in the following year, or in the Folio 1623, or, indeed, in any other ancient text; and this omission is the more observable because in all these cases the stage direction "Laertes leapes into the grave" is carefully inserted only three lines earlier. If it is borne in mind that the ordinary stage directions for this scene, with the exception noted, really possess no authority, an attentive reading of the text will, I believe, satisfy anyone that Mr. Irving is perfectly justified in not leaping into Ophelia's grave, or as the true instincts of Mr. Furnivall's "girl friends" have led them to put the case, in "not showing his love for Ophelia by stamping on her coffinless corpse with only a little mould and a few flowers over it."

I have to add that I am assured in a private note from Mr. Dutton Cook, who is probably second to no living writer in accurate knowledge of stage history, that the practice of leaping into Ophelia's grave has not been by any means so general among the Hamlets of the stage as I have assumed. Although I myself saw Macready's "farewell performance," as it was called, of this character, my recollection of this scene is somewhat imperfect; but Mr. Cook not only remembers that this distinguished actor did not leap into Ophelia's grave, but has forwarded to me a copy of Macready's acting version which directly corroborates his impression. Since this I have referred to a curious interleaved copy of *Hamlet* in my possession, in which some enthusiastic playgoer—now, I fear, far beyond the reach of my pen—has laboriously noted in pencil the "business"—as the actors say—of John Kemble in this part; and herein I find it distinctly mentioned that during the address to Laertes, "What is he whose grief," &c., "Hamlet does not advance"—the word "not" being twice underscored, as if the playgoer had there been struck with a remarkable innovation. Macready, therefore, probably followed Kemble in preference to his contemporary Edmund Kean, who certainly *did* leap into the grave, as we know from Hazlitt's observations on his performance.

* * * * * * * * * * *

I find to my surprise that, over and above the copy published by Mr. Haslewood in the *Gentleman's Magazine* in 1825, Mr. Collier has successively referred to, or published entire or in part, four if not five varying copies of this poem, as may be seen on reference to his *History of English Dramatic Poetry*, 1831; his *New Particulars*, 1836; and his *Memoirs of the Principal Actors in Shakespeare's Plays*, 1846. I find also that during this process the "elegy" has increased in interest and importance from the comparatively colourless version in eighty-two lines, published in 1825, to the final poem, full of names and striking allusions, and extending to 124 lines. That a manuscript so deeply interesting to students of Shakspere and of the history of the stage should have remained unpublished for upwards of two centuries, and should even have escaped the indefatigable curiosity of Reed, Steevens, and Malone, is sufficiently remarkable; but if during all this time five or six versions have been preserved, the fact seems scarcely less than miraculous. The marvel, however, does not end here, for these five or six copies appear not only to have come to light within a few years one after the other in the strict order of their interest and importance, but to have been all discovered by two gentlemen, Mr. Haslewood and Mr. Heber—the latter being, I presume, Mr. Richard Heber, son of the famous Bishop Heber. These are, at least, the gentlemen whom Mr. Collier names as having been in possession of the manuscripts. On one occasion, as I have already said, Mr. Haslewood was actually living when Mr. Collier publicly referred to him as having discovered "another copy," and this copy certainly contained the references to "Hamlet, &c.," which Dr. Ingleby and Mr. Furnivall regard as unquestionably forged; on all other occasions the references are to dead men, whose silence cannot be held to have relieved Mr. Collier from personal responsibility in the matter. Mr. Haslewood and Mr. Heber were intimate friends, and members of the "Roxburghe Club" famous for jocularity and good fellowship. It is just possible that these gentlemen may have conspired to play an ingenious hoax upon Mr. Collier, though as they were both ardent collectors of books and manuscripts they may of course have been themselves imposed upon. It is natural to enquire where are these five or six originals? As far as I have been able to ascertain, there is no evidence of their having ever existed except what is derived from Mr. Collier's references and Mr. Haslewood's communication to the *Gentleman's Magazine.* That the entire poem is spurious I am reluctantly compelled to say that I have not the slightest doubt.

Miss L. Toulmin-Smith's note, appended to the extract in the *Centurie* (p. 132), is as follows.

A controversy in the *Academy*, in January, 1879, as to the meaning of lines 17 to 24 of this elegy led to the discovery of the original MSS. of it in the library of the late Mr. Henry Huth, which was pointed out by Mr. Alfred H. Huth in the *Academy* of April 3, 1879. As in the first edition of the *Centurie* Dr. Ingleby declared his belief that lines 13-16, printed by Mr. Collier, were spurious, an opinion at first shared by Mr. Furnivall, it is satisfactory now to find that both MSS. of the poem are undoubtedly genuine, and acknowledged to be so by those critics (see Mr. Furnivall in *Academy* of 19 April, 1879). By the kindness of Mr. Alfred H. Huth, and of Mr. F. S. Ellis, who is preparing the Catalogue of the library, I have carefully collated both versions with the MSS., and give the dozen lines which relate to Shakespere, the rest of the poem — consisting in all of 82 lines in the octavo and 86 lines in the folio — being a eulogy upon the excellence of the acting of Burbage in general. The only sign of authorship is the letter H affixed to the title in the octavo copy. Both MSS. belonged to Mr. Haslewood, and the discrepancies between Mr. Collier's print and l. 15 ("King Lear," "creuel Moore") may be owing to the copy which an autograph note in one of them says that he sent Mr. Collier.

As to the assertion here made, that 'both the MSS. of the poem are undoubtedly genuine, and acknowledged to be so by both those critics,' I can only positively assert that I never made such an acknowledgment. For, in the first place, I have never inspected those manuscripts, or either of them; and secondly, if I were convinced of their antiquity, I should be careful to distinguish between an antique manuscript which is also probably genuine, and one which is also probably spurious.

I note here that the three versions printed by Mr. Collier are from three distinct and differing manuscripts: the lines given in his *History of Dramatic Poetry* are certainly from that in Mr. Huth's folio volume: the source of those given in *New Particulars* is at present unascertained: while the longest version, viz., that printed in *Memoirs of the Principal Actors*, &c., is from a copy made by Mr. Collier from a manuscript then in the collection of Mr. Richard Heber, and supposed at present to be at Cheltenham.

It would be 'to waste criticism upon unrelenting imbecility' to write an essay to prove either that the lines are wretched trash or that the Elegy is spurious. Mr. Fleay, in a paper on Actors, read to the Royal Historical Society, February, 1880, contains every notice of actors known from 1576 to 1642, and in *no one instance* is an actor found acting for two companies at the same date. Now Burbadge never severed his connexion with his company. He remained a member of it as Lord Strange's, the Lord Chamberlain's, and the King's Company. But in the Elegy he is represented as having sustained a number of characters in plays which never belonged to that company.

He is here said to have personated 'Antonio,' in *Antonio and Mellida*, which belonged to Paul's children: 'Frankford,' in *A Woman Killed with Kindness*, which belonged to Worcester's men: 'Brachiano,' in *The White Devil*, which belonged to Queen Anne's men: 'Edward,' in *Edward II*, which belonged to Pembroke's men. Not one of these plays ever became the property of Burbadge's company, and yet they are all alluded to in Mr. Collier's third printed version of the Elegy.

The following versions are taken, by permission of Mr. A. Huth, from the magnificent Catalogue of his Library. The first is from an octavo volume of manuscripts, the second from a quarto volume in that collection.

On ye Death of ye famous Actor
R. Burbadge.

Some skillfull limmer helpe mee, yf not soe
Some sad Tragadian to expresse my woe;
But (oh) hee's gon', yt could ye best both limne
And Act my greife, & onely tis for him
That I invoke this strange assistance to it
And in ye point call for himselfe to doe it;
For none but Tully Tully's praise could tell,
And as hee could, no man could act so well.
This point of sorrow for him none can drawe,
So truly to ye lyfe, this Map of woe,
This griefes true picture, wch his losse ha-bred;
Hees gon' & wth him wt a world are dead.
Oft haue I seene him leape into a Graue
Suiting ye person, (wch he us'd to haue)
Of a mad Louer, wth so true an Eye
That there I would haue sworne hee meant to dye

Oft haue I seene him play his part in Jest,
So liuely, yt spectators, & ye rest
Of his Crewes, whilst hee did but seeme to bleed
Amazed, thought he had bene deade indeed.
Oh! did not knowledge check me I should sweare
Euen yet it is a false report I heare;
And thinke yt hee who did so truly faigne
Is only dead in Jest to liue againe.
But now this part hee Acts not playes tis known,
Others hee plaide but now hee acts his owne
Englands great Roscius, for wt Roscius
Was more to Rome yn Burbadge was to us,
How to ye person hee did suite his face,
How did his speech become him & his pace
Suite with his speech. Whilst not a word did fall
Wthout iust weight to ballance it withall
Had'st tu but spoke to death, & used ye power
Of thy enchaunting tongue, but ye first hower
Of his assault, hee had let fall his dart
And charmed bene by all thy charming Art.
This he well knew & to preuent such wrong
First cunningly made seisure of thy Tonge.
Then on ye rest t'was easy by degrees
The slender Ivy Topps ye tallest Trees
Poets! whose glory t'was of late to heare
Yr lines so well expres't; henceforth forbeare
And write no more, or yf you doe let 't bee
In Comick scenes; for Tragic parts you see
Die all wth him; Nay rather sluce yr Eyes
And henceforth write nought else but Tragedies,
Moist Dirgies, or sad Elegies, & those
Mournfull Laments wch may expresse yr woes
Blurr all yr leaves wth blotts, yt wt is writ
May bee but one sad blacke, & upon it
Draw marble lines, yt may outlast ye Sun,

And stand like Trophies wn ye world is done.
Or turne your Inke to blood your penns to spears
To pierce & wound ye hearers hearts & eares.
Enrag'd, write stabbing lines yt euery word
May bee as apt for murder as a sword
That no man may suruiue after this fact
Of ruthlesse Death eyther to heare or act
And you his sad companions to whome Lent
Becomes more Lenton yn this Accident,
Henceforth yr wauering Flagge no more hang out
Play now no more at all; wn round about
Wee looke & misse ye Atlas of yr spheare
Wt comfort thinke you haue wee to bee there
And how cann you delight in playing when
Sad mourning so affecteth other men
Yf you will hang it out, yn let it weare
No more light colours, but Death's liuery beare
Hang all yr Howse wth Black, ye eaues it bear's
Wth Isicles of euer-melting teares.
And, yf you euer chance to play againe
Let nought but Tragedies affect yr Scene
And tu (Deare Earth) yt must enshrine yt dust,
By Heauen now committed to thy trust;
Keepe it as precious as ye richest Mine
That lies entomb'd in ye riche wombe of thine
That after times may know yt much lou'd mould
From others dust, & cherish it as gold.
On it bee laid some soft, but lasting stone
Wth this short epitaph endorst thereon;
That euery one may reade & reading weepe
Tis Englands Roscius Burbadge whom I keepe.

(Folio volume in Mr. Huth's library, first part, pp. 99–101. Variations given in the notes of the octavo MS. in the same library, pp. 174–179.)

A Funerall Ellegye on ye Death of the famous Actor Richard Burbedg who dyed on saturday in Lent the 13 of March 1618

Some skilful Limner helpe me, if not soe
some sadd Tragedian helpe t'expres my woe
but oh he's gone, that could both best; both Lime
and Act my greife; and tis for only him
that I inuoake this strange Assistance to itt
and on the point inuoake himselfe to doe itt,
for none butt Tully, Tullyes praise can tell,
and as he could, no man could act soe well.
this part of sorrow for him, no man drawe,
soe trewly to the life, this Mapp of woee
That greifes trew picture, wch his loss hath bred
hee's gone & wth him what a world are dead.
which he reuiu'd, to be reuiued soe,
no more young Hamlett, ould Heironymoe
kind Leer, the Greued Moore, and more beside,
that liued in him; haue now for ever dy'de,
oft haue I seene him, leap into the Graue
smiting* the person, wch he seem'd to haue
of A sadd Louer, with soe true an Eye
that theer I would haue sworne, he meant to dye,
oft haue I seene him, play this part in ieast,
soe liuly, that Spectators, and the rest
of his sad Crew, whilst he but seem'd to bleed,
amazed, thought euen then hee dyed in deed,
O lett not me be checkt, and I shall sweare
euen yett, it is A false report I heare,
and thinke that he, that did soe truly faine
is still but Dead in ieast, to liue againe,
but now this part, he Acts, not playes, tis knowne
other he plaide, but Acted hath his owne

* A mere slip for 'suiting.'

Englands great Roscious, for what Roscious,
was unto Roome, that Burbadg was to us.
how did his speech become him, & his pace,
suite with his speech, and euery action grace
them both alike, whilst not A woord did fall,
without just weight, to ballast itt with all,
hadst thou but spoake to death, & us'd thy power
of thy Inchaunting toung, att that first hower
of his assault, he had Lett fall his Dart
and quite been Charmed, by thy all Charm[in]g Art.
This he well knew, and to preuent this wronge
he therfore first made seisure on his tounge,
then on the rest, 'twas easy by degrees
the slender Iuy tops the smallest trees,
Poets whose glory whilome twas to heare
your lines so well exprest, henceforth forbeare,
and write no more, or if you doe let 't bee
in Commike sceans, since Tragick parts you see,
dy all with him; nay rather sluce your eyes
and hence forth write nought els but Tragedyes,
or Dirges, or sad Ellegies or those
mournfull Laments that nott accord with prose,
blurr all your Leaus with blotts, that all you writt
may be but one sadd black, and open itt
draw Marble lines that may outlast ye sunn
and stand like Trophyes, when the world is done
turne all your inke to blood, your pens to speares
to pearce and wound the hearers harts and Eares,
enrag'd, write stabbing Lines that euery woord
may be as apt for murther as A swoord
That no man may suruiue after this fact
of ruthless death, eyther to heare or Act
and you his sad Compannions to whome Lent
becomes more Lenton by this Accident,
hence forth your waving flagg, no more hang out

play now no more att all, when round aboute
wee looke And miss the Atlas of your spheare
what comfort haue wee (thinke you) to bee theer
and how can you delight in playing, when
such mourning soe affecteth other men,
Or if you will still putt 't out Lett it weere
no more light cullors, but death liuery there
hang all your house with black, the Ewe it bears
with Iseckls of euer melting teares,
and if you euer chance to play agen
may nought but Tragedyes afflict your sceane
and thou deare Earth that must enshrine that dust
by Heauen now committed to thy trust
keepe itt as pretious as yᵉ richest Mine
that Lyes intomb'd, in that rich womb of thine,
That after times may know that much lou'd mould
from other dust, and cherrish it as gould,
on it be laide some soft but lasting stone
with this short Epitaph endorst thereon
 that euery Eye may reade, and reading weepe
 tis Englands Rosecious, Burbadg that I keepe.

VI.

SHAKESPEARE'S PLAY-WORK.*

THERE is one kind of pursuit which man cannot be cured of, though it is of all hopeless things one of the most hopeless, and which can only be rewarded with the discovery of a 'mare's nest.' I do not blame my race for their pertinacity and perseverance in what I know to be a hopeless chase; for those qualities are of the highest value, and even by their misuse are not utterly wasted. But assuredly the famous knight of La Mancha never attempted anything so absurd as to surprise the secrets of Nature by analysis. Kant had arrived at a great truth when he ruled that synthesis must go before analysis, and that we can only separate where we have conjoined. Hence the futility of getting at the heart of things by dissection, whether we dissect the living organism or the dead. It was the latest French translator of Shakespeare who talked of surprising the secrets of his genius by an analytical study of the Hamlets of 1603 and 1604. Even if the Quarto of 1603 were, what it assuredly is not, a draft of Shakespeare's first sketch, it would never serve such a purpose. The secrets of genius are mainly hidden from the man himself, and he always

* Part of this essay was prefixed to Mr. Cattell's useful little work, *Great Men's Views of Shakespeare*, 1879.

does more than he knows of or knows how. No such utopia do I set myself to find in this brief essay. All I propose to show is the habit of the author and his method of composition. We cannot explain Shakespeare, nor any other genius. All that is to be explained in any literary work is the trick of it; and the great test of its quality just lies in this—that if it be a work of genius, the wonder, love, and interest it excites are just the same after the trick is exposed as before: for the trick is a mere non-essential and externality. I do not assert that there is any trick in Shakespeare's best works—if in any work of his. These geniuses are not partial to trickery, prestige, or glamour. They paint in more enduring colours. But every work of his, play or lyric, like the works of inferior artists, has in it some evidences of its production: a *navel* which shows its origin, and a *tendon* which shows where Thetis held the hero when she made him invulnerable. In the case of Shakespeare we have also evidences external to his writings which are material to a just estimate of his processes, viz., the several biographical deliverances of rare Ben Jonson. No man had a more thorough personal knowledge of the 'gentle Will' than Ben. Not only was he Will's intimate and fellow, but he possessed a genius himself which served him to judge of Shakespeare more thoroughly and accurately than we can hope to do.

The ancient opposition between business and pleasure, between work and play, which is pointed in so many proverbs, and enforced in so many moral essays, has often found itself in jeopardy from the fluctuation in the meaning of the words employed to express it. The very word which the Greeks used to convey the sense of *leisure*, the time set apart for meals, repose, or diversion, became the by-word for that work to which, through the learning and philanthropy of the philosophers, much of that time was devoted.*

One of the best among the *Proverbes of Syr Oracle Martext*† runs thus:

> There is no good worke that is not plaie,

and it is surely unquestionable that what a man does best is among the things he does most easily. On the contrary, there are men so devoid of that natural adroitness, that sense of beauty, proportion and decency, which characterise the artist, that their recreations are taken hardly, and their very prolusions are painful and laborious exercises. It is indeed a profound satire on human nature when we see men weighed down with trifles, and laboriously employed in the production of light literature.

In that prolific age of wit and wisdom, of which Marlowe gave the glorious promise, and Milton the divinest echo, the drama was scarcely regarded as the business of a profession; and the mere fact that its separate productions were called

* Mr. R. Grant White has a pertinent note in his *Shakespeare's Scholar*, 1854, p. 59. He gives several examples of the use of *leisure* in a sense apparently referring to time and not necessarily to relaxation; and in his opinion the word is so used in *Henry VIII* where the King addressing Wolsey says,

> You have scarce time
> To steal from spiritual leisure a brief span,
> To keep your earthly audit.

Adopting this view, a Greek scholar would naturally employ σχολή for 'leisure' in translating that passage.

† A small manuscript which I am editing for the press.

Plays was deemed an all-sufficient reason for distinguishing them from those serious productions which authors love to style their Works. The earliest instance of this which I have recorded occurs in one of Robert Chamberlain's *Conceits*, &c., 1639 (*Centurie of Prayse*, 2nd edition, p. 226), where it is said that Shakespeare's 'plays were worth a great deal of mony, but that he never heard, that his works were worth anything at all.' Leonard Digges in 1640 (*Centurie*, p. 231) refuses to call Shakespeare's book his 'works,'

> for to contrive a Play
> To him was none:

the notion having already taken fast hold of his countrymen, that he was the child of Nature and Fancy. H. Fitzgeoffrey, in his *Elegies*, 1618, sneeringly speaks of

> Bookes, made of Ballades: Workes of Playes;

and Sir John Suckling, in his *Sessions of the Poets*, 1646, says that Ben Jonson claimed the bays,

> For his were called Works, where others were but Plaies.*

In reference to this ancient incapacity to see genuine and genial *work* in a literary production intended to serve, or subserve, the purpose of recreation or amusement, I have called Shakespeare's industry *Play-work*. I also intend by that compound to express a characteristic which, of all poets, was pre-eminently his; viz., that he worked, not as the forger of lucubrations, nor as the founder of philosophies, but quite naturally

* See *Centurie*, p. 233, for other examples.

and easily, as Ariel raised the Tempest, or as Puck could have fabricated a girdle to clasp 'the thick rotundity of the world' in its delicate embrace. I mean the felicity and facility of production; shewing the great poet to have been a giant 'who could wield as a weapon what we can scarcely lift as a burden,' and make the highest and deepest functions of imagination and intellect the plastic instruments of his will and pleasure.

At pp. 163-4 of Mr. Swinburne's helpful and well-written essay, *A Study of Shakespeare*, we read—

> Of all vulgar errors the most wanton, the most wilful, and the most resolutely tenacious of life, is that belief bequeathed from the days of Pope, in which it was pardonable, to the days of Mr. Carlyle, in which it is not excusable, to the effect that Shakespeare threw off *Hamlet* as an eagle may moult a feather or a fool may break a jest; that he dropped his work as a bird may drop an egg or a sophist a fallacy;
>
> * * * * * * * * * * * *
>
> scene by scene, line for line, stroke upon stroke and touch upon touch, he went over all the old laboured ground again.

With all respect for this unqualified criticism, as the revised work of a man of genius, I do not feel the slightest diffidence in calling it in question. In the first place, I should impute purblindness to any critic who did not see in *Hamlet* abounding evidences of the inequality in its workmanship. When we remember that like many other plays of our author it was probably founded on one that had already possession of the stage, we can well believe that it was subjected to much revision involving numerous omissions and insertions. But I see no reason to believe that Shakespeare habitually revised his own insertions, or his own metrical expressions of a conception already worked out and selected. It seems to me a task of no great acuteness to distinguish Shakespeare's latest work in *Hamlet*, among which stands out in the most prominent relief the closet scene of the Prince and his mother. Here the rapidity of execution is evident in the rapidity of articulation; and a sense of impetuosity is imparted, which no studious elaboration of 'line upon line,' 'stroke upon stroke,' or 'touch upon touch' could achieve. If this be the case with *Hamlet*, it is likely to be so with every other play of Shakespeare's: much more, then, with the work of a lesser artist. In every dramatic or epic work, in fact in every literary composition which involves variety of treatment and distinction of parts, there will always be some irregularity in the workmanship. It is generally accepted as a critical condition, that greater polish and finish are to be required in a small than in a large poem, in a simple than in a complex work. We pass over passages and parts in the latter which we should regard as serious blemishes in the former. For this there are three sound reasons: in the briefer and simpler composition (1) the wholeness of the conception is easier; (2) the revision of the phraseology has more the character of an adjustment of ear to mind; (3) the finish or polish is attainable at a smaller relative cost—*i.e.*, the business of attaining it is necessarily less disproportionate to the end in view—than in the longer and more complex composition. There are critics who hold that this labour of revision is never out of place, and that in a drama or epic every part should be equally elaborated towards perfection. I do not take this view; nor does Mr. Ruskin. For instance, in *Troilus and Cressida*, parts have been attributed to an inferior writer because they are less powerful and finished. But those parts, though indispensable to the completeness of the play as a whole are not in themselves of sufficient importance to pay for the elaboration which has been expended on others. I say then, we must not look for equality of execution in a play; and I say further, that we do not find it in any play in the world, and that we must discount our criticism on this ground. Sir Henry Taylor, in his interesting, but not profound, *Notes on Books*, denies the possibility of an entire poem of great length: such a composition, he says, is always a connected series of small poems. Adopting this view, I would say, that any of Shakespeare's plays is not one entire work, but a scheme which connects a series of scenes. Some of the scenes demanded, and have received, the utmost possible finish—whether *tout-à-coup* or by painstaking elaboration is not yet the point—while others are loose and slipshod. We can, I think, show readily enough how this came about. In fact, this business of schematising and connecting of parts into a so-called whole was very much a matter of accident, and evidently Shakespeare was not as solicitous about it as many inferior workers have notoriously been. In modern times we know precisely how Dickens and Thackeray wrote their narrative works. To take only two of them, we have *Our Mutual Friend* and *Denis Duval* in the form of schemes, with trials of suggested variations. The conscientious discharge of this not very material duty in these cases fills me with more astonishment than admiration. I do not regret the pains bestowed on this kind of labour in the cases cited. In *Denis Duval* the effect of those pains is most curious;

for one cannot read the book without the feeling that dear old Thackeray is giving us a real bit of biography. The verisimilitude is so exact that, when one knows the process by which it was produced, its effect is rather enhanced than marred.

Shakespeare sometimes made his own scheme—sometimes took it from an earlier drama on the subject he had selected. The two best examples of this are *King John* and *Antony and Cleopatra*. The former is the result of filling in a skeleton taken from the *Troublesome Reign*, some of the infilling being but a recast or revision of the old phraseology;* the latter was Shakespeare's scheme (based on North's Plutarch), filled in with entirely original matter of Shakespeare's, and not, as sometimes in *Coriolanus*, with North's own language touched up so as to make it fall into verse. Before a play arrived at maturity it had to pass through many ordeals and vicissitudes, partly from the way in which the dramatist composed it, and partly from the exigencies put upon him by the Master of the Revels. There is one, and only one, extant drama of the period which shows the whole process of casting, recasting, censure, alteration, substitution, etc., viz., *The History of Sir Thos. More*. Here it is plain that it is an older play which is worked upon; the cancels and comments of the Master of the Revels, in this case Edmund Tylney, appear on the amended play, and the proposed changes in the text, in various handwritings, are affixed as riders to the copy. This curious and instructive manuscript was printed,

* On this question Mr. Edward Rose has contributed a most valuable article to *Macmillan's Magazine*, November, 1878, entitled 'Shakespeare as an Adapter.'

under Dyce's editorship, for the Shakespeare Society in 1844; and I trust it will not be long before it is reproduced in autotype, so that by multiplication of fac-similes we may defy the ravages of time, which have already seriously damaged and still endanger the original. I suppose a dramatist, cutting and slashing into a previous work, and writing substitutions or riders, almost necessarily works more rapidly than if he were sketching out an original play of his own. But even in the latter case, the *cadre* being settled, the work of infilling, with a man of pregnant imagination and facility of verbal expression, would go on rapidly enough—perhaps too rapidly: and this brings me to mention that the best work of genius is done in two distinct fashions.

1. There are those who work on the Horatian and Johnsonian plan of revision.

> Saepe stylum vertas, iterum quae digna legi sunt Scripturus.
>
> *Sat.* I, x, 72-3.

> No matter how slow the style be at first, so that it be laboured and accurate; * * * so that the sum of all is ready writing makes not good writing; but good writing brings on ready writing: yet when we think we have got the faculty, *it is even then good to resist it.*
>
> (*Jonson's* TIMBER. *De stylo et optimo scribendi genere.*)

In this manner worked Ben himself, Pope, Goldsmith, Gray, Southey, etc., etc., and, apparently, Tennyson and Swinburne.

2. There are those who know no such *régime*, but write from inner vision, and, as it were, inspiration, as Shakespeare, Milton, Goethe, Coleridge, Shelley, etc., etc., but probably no great poet of this day.

It is recorded of Goethe that he would seize the first scrap of paper he could find, and, writing hard and fast, sometimes diagonally across the paper, sometimes in the usual way, would thus record a finished lyric. As it was so written, so it was printed; and he rarely altered a word when it passed into a new edition. So Coleridge would wind off the finest poem; and unless it were written down at once, ere a new subject disturbed the images of his memory, it would be partly or wholly lost. Now we know that it was just thus that Shakespeare composed the pieces which constitute the infilling of his dramas. Perhaps some of his lyrics—in particular the *Phœnix and Turtle*—were written with some revision; just as Ben Jonson wrote those matchless lyrics (in his *Eupheme*), which are addressed to Lady Venetia Digby. We *feel* it must have been otherwise in Shakespeare's dramatic works from the very structure of the verses in his best plays: *e.g.*, *Measure for Measure*, *As You Like It*, *The Winter's Tale*, *The Tempest*, *Lear*, *Othello*, and the parts of *Troilus and Cressida*, *Timon*, and *Pericles*, which are attributed to him by the consensus of critics.* We *know* it was

* One passage in *Othello* is certainly not Shakespeare's. Its author was, probably, the miserable penny-a-liner who wrote the additions to Shakespeare's unfinished *Timon*: but never such atrocious stuff as for once he was permitted to write for Othello:

> *Oth.* 'Tis he:—O brave Iago, honest and just,
> That hast such noble sense of thy friend's wrong!
> Thou teachest me,—Minion, your dear lies dead,
> And your unblest fate hies: strumpet, I come!
> Forth of my heart those charms, thine eyes, are blotted;
> Thy bed, lust-stain'd, shall with lust's blood be spotted.
> (Dyce. Act v, sc. 1.)

Risum teneatis amici? For my part it is quite evident that Shakespeare did not intend Othello to speak at all. He enters at the back of the stage to take secret note of the scene.

so from the testimony of his fellows, Heminge and Condell, and from the reiterated blame of Ben Jonson. But this blame, which simply charged his friend with neglecting his own canon, and writing hastily without revision, is considerably qualified in his immortal Tetralogy on Shakespeare:

> Yet must I not give Nature all: thy Art,
> My gentle Shakespeare, must enjoy a part.
> For tho' the Poet's matter Nature be,
> His Art doth give the fashion: and that he
> Who casts to write a living line, must sweat
> *(Such as thine are)* and strike the second heat
> Upon the Muses' anvil: turn the same,
> (And himself with it) that he thinks to frame:
> Or for the laurel he may gain a scorn,
> For a good Poet's made as well as born,
> And such wert thou.

I make no question that Ben is here writing from his inmost conviction. Of course he knew 'a living line' when he saw one. He knew that he had written living lines, and he knew how he had elaborated them: not indeed with as difficult production as Goldsmith or Gray, nor yet with as fastidious revision as Pope, Southey, or Tennyson, but, as he says, by 'striking the second heat upon the Muses' anvil.' He unquestionably believed that when Shakespeare wrote at his best he did so too—only at times growing impatient of his friend's irregularity, he heartily wished his friend had been more solicitous in the work of revision. But on this point we know better: we know that Shakespeare (like many another poet) wrote at his best when he least needed revision; and that the *sufflamen* which Ben longed to put upon him would have fatally impeded the sure current of his genius. The language of Shakespeare is seldom that of a solicitous man. He bends his native English to his will in a truly marvellous manner, to a great extent constructing his own grammar, and ultimately not a little modifying that of his successors. His mighty thoughts do not wait for correct expression in the language of his forefathers, but forge their own integuments with the swiftness and certainty of a creator.

THE REST IS SILENCE.

Printed by JOSIAH ALLEN, Birmingham.

www.ingramcontent.com/pod-product-compliance
Lightning Source LLC
Chambersburg PA
CBHW020920230426
43666CB00008B/1513
* 9 7 8 3 3 3 7 0 7 4 5 9 3 *